RETURN
OF THE
JEW

JEWS OF POLAND
Series Editor – Antony Polonsky (Brandeis University)

RETURN
OF THE
JEW

. . .

Katka Reszke

IDENTITY NARRATIVES OF THE THIRD
POST-HOLOCAUST GENERATION OF JEWS IN POLAND

Boston 2013

Library of Congress Cataloging-in-Publication Data:
A catalog record for this book is available from the Library of Congress.
Copyright © 2013 Academic Studies Press
All rights reserved

ISBN 978-1-61811-308-5 (paperback)
ISBN 978-1-61811-247-7 (electronic)

Book design by Adell Medovoy
Cover design by Anna Skotarczyk and Katka Reszke

Photographs by Katka Reszke

Published by Academic Studies Press in 2013
28 Montfern Avenue
Brighton, MA 02135, USA
press@academicstudiespress.com
www. academicstudiespress.com

For S.

Contents

Acknowledgments

THIS BOOK IS THE result of research carried out over a period of ten years. Most of the fieldwork was performed as part of my doctoral program at the Melton Centre for Jewish Education at the Hebrew University of Jerusalem. I express my deepest gratitude to the Melton Centre for the kind and generous support throughout my doctoral work. I would also like to thank the Mandel Foundation for graciously sponsoring my first year at the Hebrew University.

I owe sincere thanks to the Memorial Foundation for Jewish Culture for their support during the advanced stages of my PhD work.

I am short for words in attempting to thank my two advisors. I thank Dr. Zvi Bekerman for constantly challenging me intellectually and for being an honest and patient critic and a contributor to my work. I thank Prof. Gaby Horenczyk for his priceless advice and for being my most inspiring teacher as well as a true friend. I could not have imagined having better mentors during my time at the Hebrew University.

The Melton Centre's entire academic and administrative staff provided a remarkably supportive and friendly environment throughout my doctoral years. Special thanks go to Hinda Hoffman for all her help and kindness.

I would like to acknowledge my two dear friends who have directly contributed to this book through their brilliant comments: Agata Strządała and Jaakko (Jaska) Turunen. I thank Jaska for indulging me with absurd late-night conversations in the snow-covered Helsinki, where I ended up writing most of the manuscript. I thank Agata for always being my partner in crime in our hometown of Wrocław and for being a merciless critic of everything I do or say.

I extend my thanks to a number of people I know who have inspired my work through conversation or through their writings: Helena Datner, Konstanty Gebert, Ruth Ellen Gruber, Henryk Grynberg, Staszek Krajewski, Shimon Redlich, Sigmund A. Rolat, Michael Schudrich, and Jonathan Webber. Special thanks go to Henryk Grynberg, who took the time to edit my manuscript and offered invaluable comments, as well as to Shimon Redlich and Antony Polonsky for their interest in this project and kind support during the final stages of the writing process. I am grateful to Sharona Vedol and Kira Nemirovsky for their earnest editorial work. I thank also Jan T. Gross, Jonathan Ornstein, and Piotr Nawrocki for their guidance in promoting the Polish-language edition of this book.

Thanks also to the many people whose friendship and support have made my life better during the past decade and who—*nolens volens*—contribute to my ever-shifting understanding of Jewish identity: Małgo Bakalarz, Cliff Aron, Izabela and Michael Barry, Dorota Betiuk, Danny Bluestein, Magda (Bronka) Braniecka, Kora Cecerska, Ewa Charęza, Ania Chipczyńska, Miriam Gonczarska, Rony Corcos, Elizabeth Corlin, Joanna Dyduch, Matan Fogelnest, Moshe Hayman, Sara Kagan, Agnieszka Kargol, Iga Kazimierczyk, Jan and Maciej Kirschenbaum, Michał Klajman, Monika Krawczyk, Helise Lieberman, Daniela Malec, Justyna Molasy-Dumais, Aviva Newman-Mechanic, Jonathan Ornstein, Bogna Pawlisz, Rafi Schuchat, Beata Schulman, Hana Dar Starowicz, Karolina, Robert and Lea Szykier-Koszucki, Goldie Rabinowitz-Arvatz, Menashe Tsoref, Sharon Wagner-Zauder, Jeremy Zauder, Tadeusz Woleński, Zocha Żak, Ania Zielińska, Beata Zając, Agnieszka Ziątek, and Natalia Zimnowodzka.

I remain indebted to ŻOOM—the Polish Jewish Youth Organization—and the extraordinary group of my Polish Jewish friends who have agreed to be my interviewees and whose life stories continue to help me understand the complexities of Jewish identity, including my own.

It is a pleasant duty to express my sincere thanks to Sigmund A. Rolat for his generous support in publishing this book.

I thank my family and especially my beloved maternal grandmother Stenia, who helped me discover our family's Jewish background as well as my paternal grandmother, Jadwiga, who helped us discover Jewish roots also on the other side of the family.

Finally, my most special thanks go to my parents Edward and Ryszarda Reszke for always believing in me and supporting me in all of my decisions, including the less reasonable ones, and to Sławek Grünberg for his loving support and for continuously helping me in becoming a better version of me.

INTRODUCTION

Unexpected Generation

The contemporary Polish Jewish milieu provides a unique context for the study of identity construction and cultural representations. Both Polish Jewish culture and Polish Jewish identity remain far from self-evident concepts. Jewish culture in contemporary Poland is not a returning phenomenon. It is a new construct, which very much relies on its past renderings and aspires to be rooted, to be a continuation. It has to be appreciated though that what we are witnessing in post-transition Poland is no Jewish cultural comeback but rather an ongoing struggle to construct an utterly new contemporary Polish Jewish culture. Jewish culture has been part of the Polish landscape for centuries, yet its "reappearance" after 1989 has to be appreciated as an entirely new phenomenon. The emergence of a contemporary Jewish culture in Poland provokes new questions regarding the processes of defining Jewish culture and the processes of defining Jewish identity. Unique patterns of Jewish affiliation and of identity construction, which have surfaced in the Polish context during the past two decades, generate novel analytical categories. The conventional categories of classification of Jews as an ethnic, national, religious, or linguistic minority become largely anachronistic in the context of contemporary Poland. The study of the "particularly Polish" patterns of Jewish identity construction encourages a reassessment of the dominant analytical approaches, as does the study of the "unexpected generation" of Polish Jews. The participants in this study illustrate identities in transition, identities in question, identities in discussion, and hybrid or uncertain identities, and their narratives are set against the backdrop of a unique and dynamic cultural milieu.

In this study, I examine the ways in which young adults in contemporary Poland, who discover or "stumble over" their Jewish roots, give accounts of their experience, their search for forms of Jewish affiliation, their struggle to construct models of being Jewish, and their attempts to legitimize or authenticate their belonging to the Jewish collective. It is the objective of this book to pursue an understanding of the processes and patterns involved in the construction of new Polish Jewish identities. These processes are revealed in the activity of narrating identity.

Kazimierz – The Jewish District of Krakow in 2004.

My research took place between 2001 and 2011. Semi-structured interviews were conducted with fifty young Polish Jewish adults. The conceptual and theoretical frameworks of identity, Jewish identity, ethnicity, conversion, and authenticity served as resources for both the process of data generation, in which I used them as points of reference during the interview, and for data analysis. A comprehensive analysis of the participants' narratives brought about a number of central themes and patterns, which are presented in the results section. I focus on the ways in which young representatives of the third post-Holocaust generation of Jews in Poland narrate their transition into Jewishness and the ensuing process of construction of their Jewish identities.

The individuals I interviewed for this study are young adults who can be considered members of the new generation of Jews in Poland, born in the late 1970s to the early 1990s. The focus of my research was on individuals who learned about their Jewish roots in their teens. Although a number of the people I interviewed claim that they always had an awareness of their Jewish origin, they too only began seeking a form of Jewish affiliation in their teen years. For all the interviewees, the teen years began after the democratic changes which took effect in Poland after the fall of the communist regime in 1989. It is important to emphasize that none of the participants in this study was raised in a Jewish environment; rather, they all grew up in Christian or atheist households. All of the participants in the study represent the demographic group called the *1989 generation* (Irwin-Zarecka 1990; Rosenson 1996) or the third post-Holocaust generation of Jews in Poland.

The study focuses on patterns involved in narrating identity. I analyze the ways in which people give accounts of the circumstances, events, decisions, thoughts, and dilemmas which accompany them on their way to a Jewish affiliation. I undertake to show how the words of the representatives of the third generation reveal what processes are involved in assuming a cultural legacy. This requires analyzing the conceptual and evaluative frameworks, which they resort to in the interpretation of their experience and in the construction of personal representations, including the ways ideas about culture and identity are addressed in both descriptive and evaluative terms. Finally, my analysis focuses on how the interviewees locate themselves within the socio-cultural landscape and formulate models of authentication in the context of their developing Jewish affiliations and in the pursuit of a legitimate status within the Jewish community. Narrating identity is a work in progress, and consequently, I can merely try to capture and give an account of but a fragment of the story or rather of a number of fragments of a number of stories. Common themes and patterns that emerge in the analysis are exposed here in an attempt to best represent the phenomena taking place in contemporary Poland with regard to construction of Jewishness.

The narrative dimension, which is the primary focus of my analysis, finds itself at the crossroads of the prevalent postulates nurturing contemporary identity debate. In the present volume, I examine the "lay perspectives" (Hampson 1994) which transpire in how young adult Jews in Poland look at identity and ethnicity. Through personal stories, I provide an account of the "lay theories," which implicate references to existing "formal" theoretical frameworks and dominant discourses. These references are revealed in different attempts at conceptualizing identity, that is, Jewish and Polish identity, but also identity in general. They are also manifested in individual responses to the question of authenticity. Furthermore, the particular narratives illustrate rhetorical patterns, which can be interpreted in light of the discourse of ethnic identification, along the tenets of primordialism and circumstantialism.

The concept of conversion provides another important theoretical framework. The notion of conversion holds analytical value as it proves to be an operative means of identifying different individual lay perspectives related to Jewish identity, ethnic belonging, and, most importantly, group boundaries. The idea of conversion is also directly associated with issues of authenticity. Conversion to Judaism is an important notion in the discourse of the participants, and it accounts for one of the key references, which make it possible for us to pinpoint more general approaches to Jewish identity and its boundaries.

In the subsequent parts of the introductory section, I provide the socio-historical context of this study. I then delineate our major theoretical and analytical frameworks. I discuss various approaches to the concept of identity, and I go on to present the relevant theories of ethnicity. With regard to the latter, I focus particularly on the debate on primordialism and circumstantialism. I then provide different conceptualizations of Jewish identity, which reflect different approaches to identity in general. I bring in the notion of conversion, understood not only as a religious process but also as an identity transition. Finally, I present an outline of some of the theoretical perspectives on the idea of authenticity as a subject of an ongoing debate in contemporary human sciences. The introductory section is concluded with the research question, as it emerges in light of the presented theory.

About Me

And He spoke to you and as He swore to your forefathers, to Abraham, to Isaac, and to Jacob. Not with You alone do I forge this covenant and oath but with whoever is here, standing with us today, before Hashem, your God, and with whoever is not here with us today (Devarim 29:9–14).

ACCORDING TO RASHI, THE prominent Bible commentator, "Whoever is not here" means also to include the generations of Jews who will exist in the future. Rashi's comments are based on the biblical interpretation found in Midrash Tanchuma, Nitzavim 3: "The souls of all Jews were present at the making of the covenant even before their physical bodies were created."

One might say that the stories of the young generation of Polish Jews are precisely the kind of stories that inspire such commentaries, and of course—for some—they validate the mystical message.

Perhaps a midrash like this one is in fact the only way to "explain" why so many representatives of this "unexpected generation" of Polish Jews report being drawn to the Jewishness in them before they had any awareness of it. Indeed, many of these stories of the discovery of Jewish roots, including my personal story, are admittedly—mystical skepticism aside—archetypal of those irrational "pintele yid" kinds of stories. The "pintele yid" is the phrase used to describe that mysterious "Jewish spark" or more literally "the little point of a Jew," as the Yiddish expression has it, which was inscribed at Sinai in every Jewish soul, whether present or not, whether already born or yet to come.

I grew up in a liberal Polish Catholic home. This meant that we generally attended church on holidays and some Sundays, and that my parents always passionately criticized the Catholic establishment. My most vivid childhood memory of church is the memory of how much I hated it. I guess you could say that what I prayed for most was to wake up ill every Sunday. Since I was a "good kid," I actually worried that this "allergy" to church meant that there was something wrong with me.

When I was about sixteen years old, I started "becoming Jewish." I read everything I could find in Polish and in English about Jews and Judaism, and I talked about Jews and about Judaism at home and in school. My high school friends started calling me a Jew. Some of the comments were good-humored, others were not. At home, as well as at my grandmother's home, my talking about Jews and inquiring about the family's possible Jewish roots was always surprisingly welcome. It was around the time when I realized that it was not at all common in Poland to be raised thinking that Jews are a wonderful people. I came to believe that if that was all I ever heard from everybody, on both sides of the family, there is likely a Jewish connection there.

My great-great-grandmother on my mother's side was born in Stryj, Poland, which is now in the Ukraine. Her daughter, my great-grandmother, was born in Hungary, then lived in Tschernovitz (which was then in Romania and is now in the Ukraine) and moved to Poland after the war. I was lucky enough to have known my great-grandmother. She died when I was in my early teens, and my memories of her are scarce but vivid. She was a peculiar tiny lady with a noticeably dark complexion. My mother often recalled curious childhood memories of her grandmother, my great-grandmother. My great-grandfather used to pull odd jokes on her. He would hide in the closet with a large shawl over his head and some sort of box on his forehead. He would wait for his wife to open the closet and sway before her muttering: "Sholem Aleichem, Sholem Aleichem," pretending he was a religious Jew. This would drive my great-grandma crazy; she would chase him around the kitchen with a rolling pin, yelling, "You idiot, it's not funny, what if someone sees you!?"

Everyone else thought it was funny. Everyone else also knew that my great-grandfather was very sympathetic to Jews, and the reason he made these jokes was precisely because they caused such a curiously strong reaction from my great-grandma. It took no less than a few decades before it became clear that the reason my great-grandmother was so sensitive to these jokes was that she was in fact guarding a family secret. I made it my mission to connect the dots. I interviewed other family members and discovered a number of odd rituals and customs my great-grandma used to practice. Nobody knew what they meant, and it was not until

I studied Judaism that I could actually decipher the meaning behind them. Without going into details, some of the "strange" things my great-grandmother used to do were keep her milk and meat dishes separate and follow strict rules when baking challah bread, including the laws of *hafrashat challah*—removing a piece of the dough from the batch, and covering the two challah loaves with a cloth. She had only one elusive answer to any questions her children or grandchildren asked about the obscure rules: "It's just a custom." She knew the customs from her mother—my great-great-grandmother—and in fact we suspect today that perhaps it was my great-great-grandmother who made sure that the family's Jewishness would eventually be successfully obscured. She could not have known that a few generations later I would come along and mess with her plan. After all, Great-Grandma had a point when she used to call me *meshuggeneh*, which means "crazy" in Yiddish.

During the period when I began confronting my suspicions about a Jewish family link with reality, I decided to look for "real Jews" and see what it was all about. To make a long story short, I ended up volunteering at the Jewish Congregation of Wroclaw, and I soon realized that the young Jews there were no more "real" than I was. We were all in our late teens and early twenties, and we all had a Jewish grandparent, regardless of whether we could find hard or soft evidence of it. We had all been baptized and were now determined to be Jewish and still trying to figure out what it would mean for each and every one of us. Today, over a decade later, it is fair to say that we all still ask ourselves questions about what it means to be Jewish and what is it that makes each of us Jewish, but we no longer question whether we are Jewish or not. We can all now say without hesitation that we are Jewish, and in some sense that is perhaps more identity luxury than many could hope for.

In my early twenties, I ended up immigrating to Israel, where I lived for almost five years. I like to think of Israel as a peculiar identity resort or spa. We—the third generation of post-Holocaust Polish Jews—go to Israel for a few days, weeks, sometimes years, and give our Jewish identities a vacation. In Israel, our Jewish identity is of little importance, and we don't have to represent the lost millions because they are already represented there. We can see what it's like to be Jewish somewhere where it's not such a big deal. Our identity can take a holiday from all the self-questioning. In Israel, whether we drive on the Sabbath or not is not considered vital to Jewish survival. In Israel, the general feeling is that everyone is Jewish. We are the majority there, and Jewish life can carry on without us. In Poland, we are the very Jews responsible for Jewish survival. In Israel, we are de facto Poles surrounded by "real" Jews who—unlike us—do not discuss their Jewishness every day.

Despite the difficult politics, I enjoyed living in Israel very much. I became an Israeli citizen, and it was in fact purely circumstantial that I ended up going back to Poland for a while and soon found myself living in New York City—or perhaps somewhat between Poland and New York City. But the truth is that the Israeli experience, my time as a doctoral fellow at the Hebrew University in Jerusalem, having learned Hebrew, and having lived a relatively observant liberal Modern Orthodox life there, were all part of a process of attaining a level of confidence in my Jewish identity I could never have attained otherwise. In Israel, I may have learned more than I would have learned being brought up in a Jewish environment, and in that sense I needed those years to discover what kind of Jew I could or should be. As a largely secular person today, I continue to bewilder many Jews and non-Jews alike with the fact that I continue to perform many Jewish rituals, that I shake the "four species" on the Jewish holiday of Sukkot, that I make *kiddush* over wine, or that I refuse to work on Shabbat.

My grandmother as well as my parents turned out to be fully sympathetic to my decision to pursue a Jewish affiliation, and to my amazement and pride, my parents chose to declare double nationality—Polish and Jewish—in the recent Polish national census. Interestingly, as soon as I immigrated to Israel, my grandmother on my father's side suddenly decided to mention that her father was in fact Jewish. She never felt the need to share this particular piece of information with my father: "You never asked," she replied when confronted about it. So in the end, I found Jewish roots on both sides of the family, which always makes me wonder just how many Poles there are out there who could find Jewish ancestors if they only started looking. And as such ironies of history like to have it, in 2012, as I was making the final edits to the present book, my father's ninety-two-year-old father surprised him with the following words: "I shall not take to the grave with me the secret that I am a Jew." Unfortunately, my grandfather passed away before we were able to begin to assemble the fragile pieces of his story.

In Poland, many of us will never be able to document our roots, and in that sense, our ancestors have succeeded in disguising their identity.

Yet, at the same time, we are a living proof of the fact that the identity lives on, against all odds, whether we can prove our Jewishness on paper or not. Ultimately, how much has hard evidence to do with how well we really know who we are?

I have lived in Jerusalem, and I have lived in New York—arguably the two most Jewish places on the planet. And yet, strangely, I never feel more Jewish than I do in Poland; it is against the Polish landscape that my Jewishness is revealed to me most vividly. And it is likely to stay this way. One thing I can say in all certainty after all those years is that although my Jewish identity is forever fluid, as is the nature of all identities in my view, it is by all means and above all my very own.

Our phenomenon—the unexpected appearance of a third post-Holocaust generation of Polish Jews—brings about all the fundamental philosophical questions regarding Jewish identity. It illuminates both the perceived "essence" of Jewishness, and its perceived periphery and boundaries. It offers an entirely new perspective on the question of "Who is a Jew?" and questions the seemingly most obvious truths about being Jewish. Suddenly, we have an entire generation of people who individually in some sense account for a polyphony of answers to the eternal questions of "Who is a Jew?" and "What makes a Jew?" and at the same time they question every definitive answer just by being who they are.

SOCIO-HISTORICAL CONTEXT

"BY THE TIME THE RED Army 'liberated' Warsaw in January 1945, there was nobody and nothing to liberate, except for stray dogs and rats" (Zamoyski 1987, 368). Within months, all of Poland fell prey to the communist regime. "What [. . .] happened in 1944–8 was that the Soviet Union forcibly imposed a Soviet-style communist system on Poland, regardless of the people's wishes or the country's independent interests" (Davies 1984, 3). For forty-four years since the end of World War II, the Polish experience was that of an authoritarian and practically totalitarian state. The nauseating meanders of political affairs in communist Poland fostered subsequent waves of Jewish emigration. The utter inconsistency on the part of the communist government was particularly well reflected in its policy toward Jews, whether official or covert.

Less than 10 percent of the pre-war Polish Jewish population survived the Holocaust. In 1945, some 74,000 Jews, mainly survivors, registered with the Central Committee of Jews in Poland (Polonsky et al. 1996). They were joined by approximately 200,000 Jews who repatriated from the territories of the Soviet Union. Many chose to emigrate immediately. A substantial sector of those who remained in Poland sought new hopes, some of them assuming active roles in the Stalinist regime perceived at the time as a promise of a secular paradise free of all forms of nationalisms and xenophobia, and some following other patterns of assimilation (see Redlich 2011). In the first decade after World War II, the communist government was especially sensitive to the problem of antisemitism, and perceived it as an attribute of right-wing, oppositionist tendencies within society (Cala and Datner-Spiewak 1997). While anti-Jewish assaults persisted, the ruling elite made sure its policy openly condemned manifestations of antisemitism in order to protect its image in foreign public opinion. While Jews continued to leave Poland for Western countries or for Palestine and later Israel, anti-Jewish overtones became increasingly manifest in the demonstration of society's dissatisfaction with the ruling elite.

The first serious crisis of the regime came in 1956. Stalin's death in 1953 followed by the mysterious death of the leader of the Polish communist party, Boleslaw Bierut, led to the demise of the Stalinists in Poland. Both the Soviets and the new communist leadership in Poland took the opportunity to express their concerns regarding Jewish "over-representation" in the party's ranks. In his de-Stalinization speech of 1956, Nikita Khrushchev made a point of the fact that the Polish communist leadership already had "too many Abramoviches," and although such antisemitic Soviet declarations received no official sanction in Poland at the time, the general anti-Jewish mood was already unquestionable. Along with a national revolt, which was to instill a new, Polish version of socialism, nationalist tendencies began emerging on the part of the authorities as a means of strengthening the image of the new political elite (Irwin-Zarecka 1990; Kersten and Szapiro 1993; Schatz 1991). As a result of growing anti-Jewish sentiments at the time when emigration was again permitted, between 1956 and 1959, approximately fifty thousand Jews left Poland, mostly for Israel (Schatz 1991).

Official antisemitism, which was out of the question in 1956, became a notorious motif in the Polish communist ideology of the 1960s, reaching its climax in 1968. Israel's victory in the Six-Day War in 1967 triggered the already simmering official anti-Jewish resentments. Accusing Israel of aggression and the reversal of Polish official policy, which was previously supportive of Israel, came along with a parallel change in Soviet policies (Irwin-Zarecka 1990). In Poland, the stereotypes of Jews as communists, Jews as national nihilists, and Jews as a subversive political "fifth column," were now topped with a new one—that of the Jew as Zionist, assuming Israel as his only true homeland. Hence, the Jews were now perceived as traitors to Poland and an obstacle on her glorious way to socialism. Notably, most of the Zionists Poland did have in the late sixties had by that time left for the Land of Israel, and the ideological remains of political Zionism, if at all present, were far from threatening or underhanded in the Polish context. The curious hybrid in the form of nationalist communism gave birth to an antisemitic "mutant," which was used in the power struggle for the creation of a socialist Poland relatively independent of the USSR. This led to a major campaign against all intellectual dissent. Being an essentially anti-liberal and anti-Jewish campaign, it secured the final disillusionment and once and for all shattered the belief in the emancipating capacity of the communist vision (Schatz 1991). The party's cultural policy triggered students' and intellectuals' demonstrations and protests, which the communist party's First Secretary, Wladyslaw Gomulka, was quick to attribute to "instigators" of Jewish origin. Such antisemitism and anti-intellectualism was meant to channel social discontent into popular support (Schatz 1991). Although met with some opposition from the Polish intelligentsia, the government's anti-Jewish policies were nevertheless largely endorsed by the workers and by much of public opinion. Whether convinced communists or not, and whether pursuing some form of Jewish affiliation or complete assimilation, all people of Jewish descent became targets of persecution in March 1968. Among them were even those for whom their Jewishness had hitherto been a mystery. Historians argue that the emigration "encouraged" by the events of March 1968 practically completed the "removal" of Jews from Polish lands (Kersten and Szapiro 1993). Having fulfilled their function as scapegoats in the shifting policies of the government and having been "permitted" to leave (interestingly, all those with at least one Jewish grandparent were automatically "made eligible" for emigration) and stripped of Polish citizenship, they were now to disappear also from Polish public discourse and from Polish national memory, as it was constructed along the lines of the new socialist order.

More than 20,000 Jews were forced to leave Poland as a result of the purge of 1968, leaving between 5,000 and 10,000 Jews in the country (Gebert 1994; Irwin-Zarecka 1990). However, a number of those who found out about their Jewish roots in these malevolent circumstances initiated a process of self-discovery, which proved to be of great significance for the next generation and for the Polish Jewish circumstance at large (Krajewski 2005). The complex history and the consequences of the anti-Zionist campaign remain the subject of debate and research to this day (Grabski et al. 1997; Krajewski 1997, 2005; Melchior 1990; Rosenson 1996).

Perhaps not at all paradoxically, the events of March 1968, being the most overt exposition of post-war government-sponsored antisemitism, evoked contrary tendencies on the part of the political opposition (Ury 2000). Inasmuch as for three decades following the end of the Second World War, Jews were still disappearing from Polish land, as early as in the late 1970s and throughout the 1980s, the "Jewish question" reappeared in public discourse. Significantly, this time it was addressed also from within. To be Jewish or "pro-Jewish" after the March events became a way of "defying the authorities" in the maturing struggle for a pluralist democracy (Hoffman 1992; Rosenson 1996). In 1979, the Jewish Flying University was established. Parallel to other underground educational institutions, the JFU was created to serve as a semi-clandestine study group for both Jews and non-Jews interested in pursuing knowledge of Judaism, Jewish history, and Jewish culture (Gruber 2002). The institution, which attracted 60 to 80 people, had to disband under martial law in 1981. In the absence of Jewish educational institutions and in the face of a rather limited level of communication with the older generation, the generation of 1968, as they have been labeled (Irwin-Zarecka 1990; Melchior 1990), sought knowledge of "things Jewish" in books, primarily American publications, due to the lack of such literature in Polish at that time. For some, this underground activity resulted in an emancipation from a communist, atheist background, allowing them to move toward becoming involved and sometimes observant Jews (Gebert 1994; Grabski et al. 1997).

The Nozyk Synagogue in Warsaw, Holiday of Purim 2009

The fall of the communist regime in 1989 prepared an entirely new ground for Jewish existence in Poland. Never after the political transition did official government policy discriminate against the Jews. In a form of vicious circle, however, popular anti-Jewish resentments took on a new logic, which identified political liberalism with a Jewish background (Gebert 1994). Aside from this ever-persisting popular antisemitic babble, there emerged a no less explicit tendency on the part of the government, but primarily the intellectual and artistic elites, to express active interest in Polish Jewish history and Polish-Jewish relations. Scholars and politicians began stressing the significance of Jewish culture in the Polish landscape throughout the ages. Members of the Christian intelligentsia became increasingly involved in Jewish-Christian religious dialogue, much of it owing to Pope John Paul II, who played a major role in Catholic-Jewish reconciliation in Poland and beyond. The growing interest in "things Jewish" continues to produce numerous Polish publications devoted to Jewish themes (Gruber 2002).

Immediately following the end of the war, the Jewish institutional network in Poland consisted of only two official institutions: the Jewish Central Committee in Poland, which in 1950 became the Social-Cultural Association of Jews in Poland, and the Union of Jewish Religious Congregations in Poland, temporarily renamed in the early post-war years the Union of Congregations of the Mosaic Faith (Schatz 1991). Both these establishments continue to exist today. The democratic changes with the fall of the communist regime in 1989 allowed for the development of the Jewish institutional network and for a considerable expansion of the scope of options available to individuals within that network.

We can speak of three generational groups in post-communist Poland (Grabski et al. 1997; Irwin-Zarecka 1990; Rosenson 1996). The pre-war generation of "old-timers" consists of people born before World War II, most of them Holocaust survivors. Discouraged from their Jewishness by the horrors of the Shoah and subsequently by the antisemitic riots and attacks in the early post-war years in Poland, especially the Kielce pogrom of July 1946, they were often enticed by and submissive to communist ideas (Gebert 1994). As was mentioned earlier, they often believed in the possibility of a secular, tolerant, international Poland as a project envisioned by some communist ideologists. Some Holocaust survivors had received a traditional Jewish education before the war, spoke Yiddish, and participated in Jewish ritual life, and some had been raised in relatively assimilated Polish homes, and their Jewishness was a cultural association rather than a religious one. After the war, some survivors decided to disguise their Jewish identification and similarly made no mention of it to their children. Others maintained ties with the socio-cultural association and/or with the local Jewish congregation.

The middle generation or the "68-ers" are generally associated with those Jews who left Poland as a result of the antisemitic purges of 1968 (for reference, see the documentary film *The Peretzniks* by Slawomir Grünberg, 2009). Today, the children of Holocaust survivors who remained in Poland are often labeled *Second Generation*. Whether they're called *Generation '68*, the *March Generation* (Wiszniewicz 2008), or simply the *Second Generation*, their Jewishness is largely defined by the experience of the 1968 expulsion. Those who remained in Poland and can be identified as Jews are generally people who chose to pursue a form of Jewish identity in early adulthood. Among them were those who had little or no awareness of their Jewish ancestry and who decided to learn "how to be Jewish" from foreign books and eventually became involved Jews like Konstanty Gebert and Stanislaw Krajewski, who became two of the leading Polish Jewish opinion makers and publicists in post-transition Poland. Many "68-ers" ended up joining anti-communist opposition and the "Solidarity" movement in the fight against the regime.

For the young generation of Polish Jews born after 1968, it is the year 1989, with the fall of the communist regime, that remains climactic (Gebert 1994; Gudonis 2001a; Krajewski 1997; Rosenson 1996). The shift in official policy and the spirit of democratic changes prepared the air for new attitudes toward the meaning of being Jewish and the sole idea of being anything other than Polish Catholic (Pinto 1996a,b). Whether the young representatives of this third post-Holocaust generation discovered their Jewish ancestry in their teens or had always been aware of it, it generally wasn't until the 1990s that they addressed that knowledge and initiated the pursuit of modes of Jewish affiliation. The younger representatives of this generation came of age in the first decade of the twenty-first century, and that is when they began their journey into Jewishness. The quest for forms of Jewishness enacted by "Generation '68" did not present itself as a case of direct inheritance (Gebert 1994). Similarly, the types of Jewish affiliation, which come to play in the discussion of the third generation, are scarcely indicative of adherence to the models endorsed by older generations. This generational discontinuity becomes even more striking given the fact that the parents of most of the young people I interviewed are not to be found among those who decided to embrace some form of Jewish affiliation in the period between the late 1960s and the early 1980s.

How many Jews are there in Poland today? It depends on who is asking who and who is defined as a Jew (Gebert 1994). Consequently, the answers range from a little over 1,000 to as many as 100,000. In 1996, Diana Pinto (1996b) estimated the number of members of the Polish Jewish community at 20,000. In 1999, the numbers were estimated at 5,000 to 15,000 (Sułek 1999). The Polish national census in 2002 included a question about national identification, and because Jews in Poland are in fact Polish nationals who, for the most part, identify as Poles, and the census did not include a question about religious affiliation, the number of Jews the census generated was 1,100. The fact that Jewish identification in Poland is not necessarily a national one is only one of the factors that make it difficult to estimate the number of Jews in today's Poland. Another problem is posed by the definition of Jewishness. The numbers vary greatly depending on whether we use the Orthodox halachic definition, that is, the definition according to the Jewish religious law, where being Jewish means being born from a Jewish mother, or the Israeli Law of Return definition, which grants the right to immigrate to Israel to every person with at least one Jewish grandparent. The third issue is that of mere awareness of Jewish ancestry—it is impossible to assess how many people in Poland remain unaware of their Jewish roots. Weinbaum (1998) stated that it is impossible to definitively speak of eight, ten, or even twenty-five thousand Jews in Poland. Gebert (1998) reported that the number of Jews in Poland remains between fifteen and forty thousand. In 2005, the Helsinki Federation for Human Rights estimated the Jewish minority in Poland at 7,000–15,000, living mostly in large cities (Warsaw, Wroclaw, Krakow, Lodz, Poznan, and Gdansk). In 2012, the official web site of the World Jewish Congress estimated the Jewish population of Poland at only 5,000, whereas the American Jewish Joint Distribution Committee estimated it at 25,000. Indeed, if we take into account all Poles with at least one Jewish grandparent and dare to include the ones who have yet to discover their Jewish roots, these modest numbers would need to be tripled, if not quadrupled. In 2011, when interviewed about Jewish life in Poland, the country's chief rabbi, Michael Schudrich, said, "Over the last 21 years, thousands of Poles have discovered that they have Jewish roots and nobody knows how many thousands they are." When asked how many Jews there are in Poland today, he answered, "Pick a number; double it. It is too small. I don't know, but tomorrow there will be more" (Zwalman Lerner 2011).

Most historical and sociological accounts of Jewish existence in Poland after World War II, which do not take into account the Jewish revival of the 1990s, give the impression that the Jewish story in Poland is over or about to end (Niezabitowska and Tomaszewski 1986; Vinecour and Fishman 1977; Ziemny 2000). Few publications have appeared since the 1990s, however, which highlight the cultural processes and the dynamic changes taking place in Jewish life in contemporary Poland (e.g., Cala and Datner-Spiewak 1997; Gebert 1994; Gudonis 2001a,b; Krajewski 2005; Mayer and Gelb 2002; Pragier 1992; Rosenson 1996; Weinbaum 1998). In Polish, the focus of the publications has been mostly on the socio-historical aspects. Grabski et al. (1997) offer a very general overview of Polish Jewry after the war, giving most attention to legal and demographic issues. Similarly, Datner and Melchior (1997) focus on demographic characteristics of contemporary Polish Jews as a minority group. Melchior's (1990) study of social identity of the representatives of the middle generation of Jews in Poland remains an important contribution. The issue of contemporary Jewish cultural performativity in Poland was raised in a number of significant publications (e.g., Gruber 2002; Schischa and Berenstein 2002). Jewish-Polish relations after the fall of the communist regime were addressed by both Polish and Western European authors (e.g., Krajewski 1997; Krajewski 2005; Michlic 2006; Orla-Bukowska and Cherry 2007; Pinto 1996a). Only a modest number of articles have been published since the 1990s dealing more specifically with the issue of identity of the young generation of Polish "new Jews," with their active pursuit of Jewish identity (e.g., Gudonis 2001a,b; Mayer and Gelb 2002; Pragier 1992; Rosenson 1996). There are a number of publications that appreciate the existence of the younger generation but do not actually address the topic in depth (Gebert 1994; Gruber 2002; Pinto 1996a; Ury 2000).

It is difficult to describe what democratic Poland is like. In 1984, British historian Norman Davies wrote, "[. . .] Poland is the point where rival cultures and philosophies of our continent confront each other in the most acute form, where the tensions of the European drama are played out on the flesh and nerves of a large nation. Poland is not just a clod, or even a distant promontory; it is the heart of Europe" (Davies 1984, 463). Five years later, communism in Poland fell. In fact, some would say that the war ended in Poland in 1989. Ten years earlier, the Solidarity movement initiated the biggest revolution in the communist sector of Europe. Some argue that this secured the first and only successful uprising in Polish history (Surdykowski 2005), although many would see it as a rhetorical overstatement.

The participants in this study are people born in a country with a long and complex history of oppression. In other words, most of the participants in the study, including myself, were born in an authoritarian regime. Today, more than two decades into the new Poland, my interviewees represent an erratic generation that produces decadent malcontents (Melosik and Szkudlarek 1998; Świda-Ziemba 2005). They are too young to have had the opportunity to fight for capital F freedom, to have had the opportunity to make a difference on an international scale, and to have had that opportunity their fathers' generation had. In this study, I want to give an impression of the collective experience of the contemporary generation of young Polish adults. Of course, it is impossible to responsibly declare that all of my interviewees' fathers were freedom fighters and none of them supported the communist government, albeit passively.

It is important to note that during the 1980s, and perhaps beyond, associating oneself with the Catholic Church was tantamount to associating oneself—even if merely symbolically—with political opposition. Many Poles of Jewish origin found themselves fighting the regime, and for some this meant associating with the Catholic establishment. For those who "stood up," it meant to be on the side of the "good guys," and it meant to be part of a dangerous struggle for individuality, justice, and freedom. Because the regime represented anti-culture, those who fought against the regime used culture as a self-liberating, dignifying tool. There were of course those who supported the communist way, despite the growing disenchantment and although the communist ideal lost all of its charm in reality (Schatz 1991). It was often beneficial from a financial or practical point of view to conform with the regime, just as it might have been a safety precaution. However, those who chose to rebel against communist oppression were often extremely determined—at the symbolic level as well—to make every effort to defy the authorities, regardless of the dangers such actions could pose for them. As reported by several representatives of the third generation, some parents—regardless of their Jewish and often secular backgrounds—saw fit to baptize their offspring purely as an act of defiance against the very aggressively anti-Catholic communist regime.

The identity stories of the representatives of the third generation are diverse. It is, however, significant that their Jewish experience is situated in a relatively new and still somewhat perturbed democracy. Allow me to remark that the general assessment among the young Polish Jewish adults is that they are "children of the revolution" who came of age in the newly liberated Poland. When we look at the young generation, we see that some remember communist times better than others, some remember their fathers' political imprisonments, and some remember only the empty shelves in grocery stores. No matter how dramatic or how prosaic the individual experiences might have been, as a generation they are children of dangerous or challenging times. They are adults, however, in times of relative social and political ease, where participating in culture is no longer part of the underground and where pronouncing their opinion is not likely to get them arrested.

Polish sociologist Świda-Ziemba (2005) speaks of "The New World" (*Nowy swiat*), which was established with the fall of the communist regime in 1989. What is important is that post-communist "New World" is the natural world for the young Polish adults of today; it is the world as they know it. Świda-Ziemba's research indicates that one of the characteristics of the generation of people who came of age in post-transition Poland is in fact a striking lack of generational awareness. This is expressed in individuals denying the fact that they belong to a certain historically and socially defined group. The young adults who participated in Świda-Ziemba's study talk about an endless multiplicity of possibilities, and they describe it in negative terms: disorienting, confusing, and empty. Along with general pessimistic attitudes comes the notion of freedom of choice: freedom to choose from among these multiple possibilities is described as an imprisoning emptiness. In other words, even freedom falls victim to cynicism. "Most of us are skeptical, cynical and . . . miserable," says one of the participants in the study (Świda-Ziemba 2005, 23). Another person describes the condition in the following way, "We are a handicapped generation, because we don't know how to rebel. We can no longer fight for new civil liberties, because we already have complete civil freedom" (Świda-Ziemba 2005, 19).

Notwithstanding, it seems important to mention that perhaps especially during the past decade, a new context emerged wherein young Poles including—more significantly for this study—young Polish Jews do engage in a fight. The growing visibility of the Polish Lesbian, Gay, Bisexual, Transgender, and Queer (LGBT&Q) community has led young Polish Jews to rather poignant expressions of a sense of solidarity and a willingness to join in the struggle for equal civil rights. In the past years, a growing number of Jews, often identified by an Israeli flag, joined the LGBT&Q activists at demonstrations, protest marches, and equality parades organized every year in several large Polish cities. Common workshops are organized by the two communities, and more and more frequently they join each other's efforts in everyday protests or appeals against discrimination, racism, antisemitism, or homophobia. Many young people, among them Jews, in fact argue that—from a legal point of view—the situation of gays and lesbians in Poland is inferior to that of the Jews. For example, anti-Jewish speech is explicitly illegal in Poland, whereas homophobic hate speech is not, as of 2011. From a sociological point of view, comparing the situation of Jews and non-heteronormative persons in Poland since the fall of communism presents itself as a fascinating exercise which illuminates the complex processes of liberalization and pluralization of that part of Europe. In the Polish parliamentary elections of 2011, unexpectedly, the new political party of Janusz Palikot, who promised a liberal, anticlerical, pro-European, and pro-gay approach, was elected to the parliament having received votes primarily from young people, from the LGBT&Q community, and—interestingly—from the country's Jews. As a result, the Polish Parliament welcomed its first openly gay male MP, Robert Biedroń, and its first transgender female MP, Anna Grodzka, who is currently the only transgender MP in the world.

In this book, I deal with a specific group of young adults in Poland, and their experience accounts for an exceptionally poignant phenomenon in that part of Europe, but that experience must surely be contextualized. It must be appreciated that young Polish adults who pursue a Jewish identity do so in the socio-historical context of a post-transition system and in the context of a country which engages in a very compelling debate not only on its Jewish past and present but also on its Catholic identity and its various persisting and ceasing xenophobias.

Heterogeneity is described as one of the generational characteristics of the third post-war generation, or better yet the "non-generation." Once again, Świda-Ziemba's study reveals a peculiar paradox in the reports of the young adults. Namely, on the one hand, they talk about a unified picture of a generation as a sad victim of postmodern civilization, whereas on the other hand, the main features of this generation are described as heterogeneity, pluralism, and individualism. The general impression, as concluded by Świda-Ziemba (2005), is that we are looking at a group of people where everyone is on his or her own and everyone has to make it in this world of no authorities. All this is in many cases accompanied by a mythologized vision of the past and a certain nostalgia for the metaphysical, the existential, and the profound, which interestingly enough are perceived as characteristics of the past exclusively (Świda-Ziemba 2005). In a sense then, one of the things that the present condition has to offer to the third post-war generation is the possibility of turning to the past.

The Contemporary Polish Jewish Cultural Milieu

OVER THE PAST TWO decades, thousands of Poles discovered that they have Jewish roots. Simultaneously, thousands of Poles discovered a strong interest in what we may generally label as Jewish culture. This means that the representatives of our third generation, who are embracing Jewish identity in contemporary Poland, are doing so in the peculiar reality of a Jewish cultural transformation happening in that part of Europe. The latter is subject to much controversy, which circles around the questions of authenticity and the complexities involved in defining Jewish culture. Nevertheless, today's Poland hosts probably more Jewish culture festivals than any other country in Europe, and the number of Jewish themes addressed in the arts and media is constantly growing, and this cannot be of no significance to the growing number of people who choose to identify as Jews.

In this study, I try to provide some insight into the mysterious world of the "unexpected generation" of Polish Jews, which began to emerge in the last decade of the twentieth century. At the same time, I address the incredible eruption of artistic campaigns and enterprises that popularize Jewish culture in Poland and create a new reality, which provokes a debate on both the real and the imaginary "return of the Jews."

For most Jews, Poland signifies more than just a country. A significant percentage of the world Jewish population, including approximately 75 percent of American Jews, trace their roots to Poland (Gruber 2002). Nevertheless, the image of Poland which remains the dominant one among Jews in other countries is that of a graveyard. Poland was home to the largest Jewish community in pre-war Europe, but it was also where the worst horrors of the Holocaust happened. Poland can never be "normal" for Jews. Not for the Jewish visitors, but perhaps not even for the local Jewish population. Nevertheless, the pursuit of some kind of "normalcy" by Jews living in Poland is an important and fascinating process. To allocate and establish oneself within a landscape as complex as the Polish one is one of the central challenges for Polish Jews and—arguably—especially so for the younger generation.

Some of this "Jewish roots mania" in Poland can be attributed to the work of the American-born Michael Schudrich, who began working in Poland in 1990 on behalf of the Ronald S. Lauder Foundation. Schudrich served as rabbi of Warsaw and Lodz since 2000, and was appointed Chief Rabbi of Poland in 2004. For the past two decades, Rabbi Schudrich has been one of the pillars of the Jewish revival in Poland, and he is partly responsible for the growing number of younger Polish Jews "coming out of the closet" in Poland. As a counselor for many young Poles who have just discovered their Jewish roots, Schudrich has been able to attract and accommodate some of those who are now the representatives of the third generation. Serving as an Orthodox rabbi, he necessarily is more likely to accommodate those who pursue an observant Jewish life, but his undeniable charisma causes many to "stick around" despite their lack of interest in religious practice. And as such, his role in the processes I discuss in this book is unquestionable. As is the role of such philanthropies like the Lauder Foundation and the Joint Distribution Committee whose support for Poland dates back to the 1980s, and more recently also organizations such as Shavei Israel. The impact of these foreign philanthropic organizations on the development of Jewish communal networks in Poland cannot be overestimated.

Jewish Culture Festival in Krakow 1999.

For half a century between 1939 and 1989, being Jewish in Poland was not the most coveted identity. Since 1989, the number of Jews in Poland is actually growing, and deassimilation is at its best. Whereas for decades, many Jews in Poland pursued different forms of assimilation, since the 1990s assimilation is in reverse. Jews in Poland are "coming out of the closet." In a society where they had achieved a good level of "passing," of not being identified as Jews by others, they nevertheless "come out" as Jews publicly (see Stratton 2000).

Historians have repeatedly announced the end of Polish Jewry, and yet they—the unexpected "remnants"—now mostly in their 20s and 30s, take pride in calling themselves Polish Jews. The relationship between Poles and Jews has always been "special," whether good, bad, or just plain weird. This new generation is a generation of people who literally embody the relationship between Poles and Jews—they all epitomize Polish-Jewish relations. It is in this strange land, cursed and beloved by so many Jews, where Jews are cursed or beloved by antisemites or philosemites, respectively, that this generation of "neo-Semites" began to emerge in the last decade of the twentieth century, a generation of people who for the most part grew up as "regular" Polish Catholics but somehow ended up stumbling over their Jewish roots. Who would have thought that in this anguished land young people would pay so much attention to a heritage so many other young people have tried to escape throughout history? Why is it that the biggest insult for young Polish Jews is to be called "not real Jews"? What is even more remarkable is that all of this takes place in the context of a country which produces more Jewish festivals and art projects than any other country in Europe. Nearly every Polish city now holds a Jewish culture festival of some sort, and almost every day a Polish Jewish subject is brought up in the media. Polish-Israeli student exchanges take place every year, concerts of Jewish music happen all over the country, and a state-of-the-art Museum of the History of Polish Jews is supposed to launch in Warsaw in 2013. This museum will be a product of cooperation between Jews and Poles, both creative and financial. Poland is considered one of the most pro-Israel countries in the European Union. Moreover, the fact that it does not cease to produce overwhelming numbers of Jewish art and culture projects creates an entirely new reality—an impressive "virtual Jewish world" (for a fascinating analysis of this phenomenon, see Gruber 2002). There isn't a week or perhaps a day in Poland without a "Jewish event" happening somewhere. A "Jewish renaissance in Poland" has made international news. The *New York Times* publishes articles about non-Jews reviving Poland's Jewish culture. So where, in all of this, are the Jews?

Perhaps the best representation of the "Jewish revival phenomenon" is the annual Jewish Culture Festival in Krakow—the largest Jewish culture festival in Europe. There, for one week, the organizers try to popularize the more attractive elements of Chasidic culture, with Klezmer music, traditional dance, and kosher-style food. Over the past twenty years, a great deal of attention has been paid in Krakow to rediscovering the city's "lost" Jewish culture and promoting it to a non-Jewish public (Gruber 2010). Numerous Jewish lecturers and performers are invited to the Festival every year, but the vast majority of the "consumers" are Poles with no Jewish roots. Crowds of people can be observed in Krakow every year dancing hypnotically in the streets of the former Jewish district. The revival of "some kind of Jewish culture" in Poland is unquestionable, but how alive and how "real" are the actual Jews?

Diana Pinto (1996a) points out that European Jews must make efforts to locate themselves within the landscape of Jewish cultural performativity, which is largely managed by non-Jews in Europe. In other words, they must decide whether to be part of it or to disassociate themselves from it, and whether to try to take advantage of it or avoid being affected by it. The strategy of the third generation regarding the Krakow Jewish Culture Festival is quite curious. Namely, they use it as a pretext to gather in Krakow from all over Poland and, rather than participate in the festival's program (aside from selected concerts by guest artists from abroad), organize their own alternative get-togethers and parties. They admit that the festival provides a special, somewhat surreal atmosphere, where for one week they are surrounded by Jewish or Jewish-like "things"—music, art, dance, food, books, posters, and so on. One of the institutions which helps organize some of the alternative activities for young Polish Jews during the time of the festival is Krakow's Jewish Community Center (JCC) run by the New York–born Jonathan Ornstein. The JCC organizes parties, lectures, and Shabbat meals during the festival, and the events are mostly run by Jews, for Jews. Non-Jews are welcome, as is the policy of the JCC on a regular basis. Since 2010, young Polish Jews have organized multiple lectures and workshops at the JCC which have become integrated in the Festival's program, and this is a good example of Jews becoming more involved in creating the Festival together with non-Jews. The Krakow JCC is the best representative of a growing tendency among young Polish Jews to become visible in the urban artistic and intellectual landscape and to try to engage the city's population in Jewish activity. "In terms of the way the Jewish community interacts with the non-Jewish community and the direction that things are going"—Ornstein told Ruth Ellen Gruber in an interview in 2011—"I think that there's never been a more optimistic time to be Jewish in Krakow than there is now. [. . .] The powerful message is that Judaism isn't just an idea, it's not just something that belongs to the Polish past, but there are Jews living here." What Jonathan believes, as noted by Gruber, is that "however small their numbers, Jews in Poland are not a separate, exotic entity but part and parcel of 21st century Polish society" (Gruber 2011).

Being an event created and originally organized by non-Jews and thus criticized by local and foreign Jews with regard to its authenticity, the Krakow Jewish Culture Festival cannot be denied a positive and good-humored quality, which attracts also the Jewish visitors. Such a relative balance of commercialism and quality content can no longer be found during the "Singer's Warsaw" Festival in the country's capital, which in turn is organized by the Jewish-run Shalom Foundation. The predominant style of Jewish culture presented at the festival is similar to that of Warsaw's Jewish Theater, which is, interestingly, run by the same family. How the Jewish Theater survived the removal of practically all Jewish institutions as part of the 1968 purge is no mystery to the better informed. Why the theater's audience, just like the majority of Singer's Warsaw Festival, is predominantly non-Jewish is even less mysterious. The theater's performances, featured in parts also during the festival, have been described as "A case of art trying, unsuccessfully, to imitate art, [. . .] moaning and swaying actors and actresses trying to ape Hasidim, [. . .] non-Jewish actors in a Jewish theater, transmitting antisemitic stereotypes—in Yiddish—to the young generation of Poles!" (Hoffman 1992, 247 via Gruber 2002). Needless to say, the third generation of Polish Jews largely disassociate themselves from the Warsaw festival.

The Jewish Motifs Film Festival organized in Warsaw since 2003 is another example of a venue which attracts many Poles and Poles of Jewish origin, and it has become a valued site in the landscape of contemporary Jewish cultural activity in Poland.

Filmmaker Slawomir Grünberg at the Jewish Motifs Film Festival in Warsaw in 2008.

Another successful enterprise worth mentioning is the *Simcha* Jewish Culture Festival organized in Wroclaw since 1999, which has over the years become a much respected and popular annual event in the "Polish Jewish calendar." Since 2008 Poland has its own Limmud Conference—now the largest Jewish event in the country—where everyone is a student and anyone can be a teacher. Some 350 participants enrolled in 2008. Four years later, in 2012, Limmud Keshet Poland, which is organized by the American Jewish Joint Distribution Committee, is said to have hosted as many as 800 participants.

Another sphere of the Polish cultural milieu which affects local Jews, whether they want it to or not, is the growing number of Jewish-themed artistic enterprises and projects. Allow me to mention only a few. In 2007, Israeli multimedia artist Yael Bartana initiated the project "And Europe Will Be Stunned." The project consists primarily of three video installations and the establishment of a somewhat ambiguous movement known as the Jewish Renaissance Movement in Poland. The manifesto featured in this multimedia project calls for the return of 3,300,000 Jews to Poland—the land of their forefathers. The movement, with its appeals for more than three million Jews to come back to Poland, is an artistic invention. However, the scope of its influence has created a new reality—it is bewildering, to say the least, to both Poles and Jews. It has many debating, it has Polish antisemites protesting, and it has Polish philosemites excited. Polish Jews have yet to agree on how they feel about it. The eternal question "But is it good for the Jews?" comes to play also with regard to projects like "I miss you, Jew" ("Tesknię za Tobą, Żydzie"), which was launched by the Polish artist Rafal Betlejewski. Betlejewski appeals to the Polish public to send in any memorabilia and memories of Jews who once lived in places where they are no longer. The roots of this project go back to 2000, when Jan Tomasz Gross (2001), the Polish-born history professor at Princeton University, published *Neighbors: The Destruction of the Jewish Community in Jedwabne, Poland*. The book talks of the infamous massacre of Polish Jews in the village of Jedwabne, which was perpetrated by Poles and not by German occupiers, as had previously been assumed. The intellectual turmoil Gross caused in Poland cannot be overestimated. Finally the Polish public discourse opened itself, or was forced to open itself, to the most disturbing facts in Poland's anti-Jewish record, and while it stimulated antisemitism where it had been invisible, it brought about an invaluable reformation of national awareness at large. Polish intellectuals, some of them Jewish, others not, have written about the darkest chapters in Polish Jewish relations before Gross, but it was his uncompromising rhetoric and his compelling call for a new historiography that instigated a revolution in Poland (Orla-Bukowska and Cherry 2007).

It is perhaps this revolution that yields the many controversial art projects, which in different ways try to deal with the brutal confrontation with the most shameful chapters of Polish history. The idea of the project "I miss you, Jew" was simple. First, a list was compiled of cities and towns across Poland, which once had large Jewish populations. Betlejewski then visited those places and took photos of individuals and groups standing beside an empty chair with a skull cap on it as a sign of Jewish absence. A major event in Betlejewski's project was the 2010 public burning of a barn, meant to commemorate the Jedwabne massacre, in which Polish villagers burned their Jewish "neighbors" in a barn. The event caused much controversy and protests on the part of both Poles and Jews.

It is also in that same Poland that one can observe numerous vendors line up little clay, porcelain, and wooden figurines and memorabilia in their gift shops and market stands, among which the most valued souvenirs are tiny figurines shaped like "traditional" Jews. Large-nosed with sidelocks, accompanied by a fiddle, a book, or a cane, they are often also holding or standing by a Polish penny coin—the one grosz. Known in Polish folklore as good luck charms, relentlessly popular all over the country, sold by street vendors oblivious to the very unfortunate endorsement of notorious stereotypes, the "little Jews"—as they are called unconcernedly—crowd up next to little angels and dwarfs waiting for tourists and passers by. Once again, this "virtual Jewish presence" in Poland must be appreciated as a factor in the way Polish Jews see themselves and narrate their experience.

Another phenomenon, which is of significance especially for the younger generation of Jews in Poland, is Jewish tourism. As was mentioned before, the image of Poland as a massive Jewish graveyard shared by many foreign Jews necessarily shapes much of interaction they have with the representatives of the local Jewish community. Jewish American and Israeli visitors, most of whom come to Poland to see Nazi death camps, do not try to hide their astonishment when they realize that there are in fact Jews still living in Poland, including younger ones, and are similarly shocked at the fact that they actually choose to live in Poland rather than emigrate. Many are perhaps even more amazed at the fact that they meet young people who call themselves "Jews," although they did not grow up Jewish and do not have two Jewish parents. I address this issue further in my analysis of the interviews conducted with representatives of the third generation.

Along with the visibility of Jewish "things"—festivals, publications, concerts, exhibitions, films, and grand projects such as the Museum of the History of Polish Jews, which is bound to make a big impact on Polish society, the visibility of actual Polish Jews also advances. This mosaic of Jewish-themed activity in Poland can create the impression that there is in fact a Jewish return taking place here—that Poland is undergoing a curious transformation and becoming—in many ways—more and more Jewish. The "invasion" of "Jewish things," the outspoken invitations voiced by artists for Jews to return to Poland, and the slow process of local Jews becoming more and more visible—all of this creates an almost surreal fantasy. Thus, the specific Polish cultural milieu, with all of its idiosyncrasies, necessarily conditions the processes of identity construction and the narratives of the third post-Holocaust generation of Jews in Poland.

THEORETICAL FRAMEWORK

IDENTITY

IDENTITY IS ONE OF the central concepts in the present study. I outline the major themes in the theoretical perspectives on the question of identity, which emerged throughout the modern and postmodern times.

The central idea underlying the modern condition is the idea of individuality and modern identity construction, and it is rooted in the process of individualization. In the mid-nineteenth century, British philosopher John Stuart Mill (1869) spoke of individuality as the capacity to use our faculties in individual ways, to choose our life plan for ourselves, and not to merely be shaped by the constraint of political or social sanction (Mill 1869; see also Appiah 2005). The Ghanaian-British-American cultural theorist Kwame Anthony Appiah discusses two rival pictures of the way in which individuality is shaped. One derives from romanticism as the idea of finding one's self, which is supposedly already there, just waiting to be discovered. In other words, it is a matter of being true to who one already really is (Appiah 2005). Appiah calls it the "authenticity model," which can be somewhat confusing in that it assumes a very specific and unambiguous understanding of authenticity. Because authenticity will become one of the concepts subjected to extensive discussion later in this study, it seems both helpful and adequate to refer to Appiah's "authenticity model" as the "essentialist model." The term seems fit given the fact that the other model discussed by Appiah is called the "existentialist" one. Here, "existence precedes essence: that is, you exist first and then you have to decide what to exist *as*" (Appiah 2005, 17). Although the first approach allows little or no creativity, the second one in its most extreme version consists of "making a self up" as if out of nothing. The middle approach, as Appiah concludes, would be that it is a good thing to be constructing an identity, but only granted that it makes sense. And an identity making sense can only be secured by facts, which are beyond individual choices (Appiah 2005).

It would seem that a self that "makes some kind of sense" is one that is constructed in response to circumstances and is a product of constant interaction between a person and the world outside him or her (Burr 1995). Mill also described the "character of man" as one that is shaped between constructive will and existing in particular circumstances (Mill 1884).

We might say then that individuality happens in interaction and not in abstraction. People may be capable of making choices, but there is an extent to which such choices are conditioned or determined by existing circumstances. And this is precisely one of the central predicaments of human existence in the modern world. It is also one of the main factors in building theories of identity. And it is a constant philosophical concern throughout this study.

The rise of the modern discourse of identity can be explained in terms of a response to the dethronement of a particular idea of culture. Before that, anthropologists commonly held an understanding of culture as a collective, uniform whole, as a regulating, normative system, which determines individuals. Such individuals were perceived to be bearers of the given culture, born into it and acting according to its norms (Boas 1940; Levi-Strauss 1963–1976; Mead 1964).

The existence of late modern societies, pluralism, and multiculturalism can all be held responsible for the final crisis of the normative conception of culture and the development of an idea of culture as unstable, fragmented, heterogenic, and a subject of constant negotiation (Burszta 2004). Today, such perspectives on culture are generally identified as representative of the postmodern view. In this understanding, culture is not a wholesome unit, but rather is subject to reinterpretation and change, and individuals are free to choose their own ways of participating in it (Berger 1979; Castells 1997; Clifford 1988; Gergen 1991; Nagel 1994). Consequently, it can be argued that identity as a concept became attractive precisely because of the crisis of the concept of culture (Bauman 2001; Burszta 2004; Clifford 1988). It has been noted that "the age of identity" has come "upon us" (Bucholtz and Hall 2005, 608).

If culture no longer has the power to explicitly define human beings, or if we can no longer verify just how much authority culture has on us, then identity becomes the new key word. We could say then that the focus shifts from talking about people and their cultures to talking about individuals and their cultural identities. Once again, our underlying ideas of personal autonomy and of individualization prove to be crucial. "What the idea of 'individualization' informs of is the emancipation of the individual from his or her ascribed, inherited and inborn determination of social character: a departure rightly seen as the most conspicuous and seminal feature of modern condition" (Bauman 2001, 474). Such a shift of focus can also be observed in the Jewish context, where talking about Jewish culture necessarily brings about an often more complex discussion about Jewish identity or—better yet—Jewish identities in the plural.

If culture no longer authoritatively defines who I am, then what or who does? It must be made clear here that the idea of personal autonomy, which the idea of identity stems from, makes sense only in the context of culture. Autonomy requires choosing, and culture is what provides a kind of repertoire, a context of choice. Only through culture do people acquire a sense of the options available to them to choose from. In other words, culture provides the lens through which people identify experiences as valuable to them (Appiah 2005; Kymlicka 1991; Margalit and Raz 1990; Mead 1964; Taylor 1989). Particular cultural belonging is like oxygen—it is there, one cannot not breathe it (Tomasi 1995). This, however, should not mean that people are not capable of recognizing, appreciating, or even choosing values of cultures other than their primary ones.

Allow me to juxtapose two established schools of thinking about identity in contemporary social sciences. The distinction I want to emphasize will in fact be parallel to the distinction between two different conceptualizations of culture mentioned earlier. The first understanding of identity I wish to portray is one which stems from developmental psychology. It is generally associated with Erik Erikson (1968), who was one of the first theorists to explore the notion of identity extensively and to emphasize the role of the social aspect of an individual's psychology (Schachter 2005a). Erikson described identity as "a subjective sense of an invigorating sameness and continuity" (Erikson 1968, 19). "Sameness and continuity" demand a harmonious state of self-consistency, coherence, and stability as the guarantors of psychological well-being (Erikson 1968; see also Schachter 2005a). The Eriksonian sense of sameness and continuity is described as unfolding epigenetically, from within and according to an innate timetable (Schachter 2005b). Erikson talked about "identity achievement" as a mark of maturity. He believed that an "identity crisis" would commonly precede the adolescents' eventual maturation. In this view, identity crisis would mean a temporal loss of sameness and continuity, which is perceived to be a pathological condition requiring medical intervention (Erikson 1968; see also Bauman 2001). The expected course of development here, according to Erikson, is to overcome the period of crisis through an exploration of alternatives followed by a choice, which allows an identity closure and secures a stable, self-consistent adulthood (Erikson 1968; Schachter 2005b). Other theories of identity were developed on the basis of Eriksonian psychology. Baumeister and Muraven (1996), for example, claim that it is a task of adolescence to develop an adult identity, which then needs to continue to adapt to social environment. This comes across as another developmental theory, where the idea of progress is realized through the pursuit of a more developed, "better" identity. In this sense, for a young adult to become someone or—as is relevant in our context—to become a Jew without the basis of a Jewish childhood and adolescence would hardly guarantee a "stable," "well-developed" identity. I will try to challenge this type of thinking, focusing on the constructed nature of identity appreciated as an unfinished process.

The prominent cultural theorist Stuart Hall (1992) offers a threefold distinction of conceptions of identity. The first understanding of identity is what he calls identity of the "Enlightenment subject"—the "essence" of a unified individual who is born with an inner core which unfolds through life but nevertheless remains stable and virtually "the same." The second view is that of the identity of the "sociological subject," where more emphasis is put on the interactive nature of an individual's identity as it is construed in a dialogue with society and cultural worlds and through the internalization of socially significant meanings and values. Although the importance of a dialogical exchange between an individual and a society is accentuated, this view of identity nonetheless assumes an inner core or essence, a "center" of a person. The third conception of identity mentioned by Hall is that of the "postmodern subject." Here, no "essential identity" serves as the center of an individual, and no identity is permanent or fixed. The postmodern subject is fragmented, and the postmodern identity is multiple, flexible, and ever shifting (Hall 1992; Simon 2004). I will try to show the relevance of this perspective on identity as it is reflected in the identity narratives analyzed in this volume.

The "Enlightenment theories" and the "sociological subject" theories, as well as the middle-ground Eriksonian theory, all continue to be widely criticized as anachronistic vis-à-vis the "postmodern condition." Be that as it may, it seems reasonable to appreciate a major shift that took place in our understanding of the world and of human existence rather than to accuse older theories of being inapplicable or insensitive to newer circumstances (Schachter 2005a). That shift, it must be said, is a shift toward a fundamentally different worldview. What happened?

First, new social and cultural contexts for the development of identity have become subjects of discussion in the postmodern perspective. Second, new theoretical frameworks became prevalent as more relevant to the postmodern condition (Schachter 2005b). Schachter (2005b) gives an example of the difference between the modernist and the postmodern approach to identity. The modernist Eriksonian approach on disparate identity elements suggests that one must either choose between them or integrate them toward a structure defined by sameness and continuity (Erikson 1968). The postmodernists, on the other hand, would refrain from integrating disparate elements in an appreciation of multiple changing identities. The latter are not just accepted but in fact celebrated, as contributing to a flexible view of personality (Melosik and Szkudlarek 1998; Schachter 2005b).

The postmodern belief is that because social reality changes so rapidly and new phenomena and circumstances relentlessly challenge the individual, sameness, coherence, or stability are practically impossible to achieve for an individual and in fact perhaps not so much desired (Burszta 2004). Robert Jay Lifton (1993), one of the main theorists of postmodern identities, claims that people structure a fluid, constantly changing identity with multiple, often contrasting elements, and notes that while continuous self-recreation of identity "is by no means without confusion and danger, it allows for an opening out of individual life, for a self of many possibilities" (Lifton 1993, 4–5). Relating to classic identity theory, Lifton concludes, "I have come to see that the older version of personal identity, at least insofar as it suggests inner stability and sameness, was derived from a version of traditional culture in which relationships to symbols and institutions are still relatively intact—hardly the case in the last years of the twentieth century," and may we add, hardly the case in the narratives of the third post-Holocaust generation of Jews in Poland. The individual stories described in this book are in and of themselves endorsements of the notion of "a self of many possibilities."

The question remains: if a sense of an unalterable essence of the self, self-consistency, and coherence are no longer the desirable goals of an individual's identity, then what is? Here, again, the focus shifts from talking about identity goals or achievements to talking about processes involved in the making of an identity, about identity dynamics, and perhaps most importantly about identity construction. The idea of constructing identity was put forth by the school of social constructionism. It is an approach that challenges essentialist categorizations and emphasizes the role of multiple discourses involved in the building of identity (Burr 1995; Davis 1991; Goffman 1974; Nagel 1994; Waters 1990). Identity here is seen in terms of multiple selves as indeterminate texts created and recreated through social discourse (Gergen 1992). Identities can be multiple, shifting, and contradicting, and they are never given, stable, ready, or determined. Hall (1996) writes that what identity does not signal is a stable core of the self, unfolding from the beginning to the end through the vicissitudes of history without changing. Along similar lines, sociologist Anthony Giddens (1984) maintains that in the post-traditional order, self-identity is not inherited or static. Rather, it becomes a reflexive project—an endeavor that we continuously work and reflect on. It is not a set of observable characteristics of a moment, but it becomes an account of a person's life. A self-identity has to be created and continuously reordered against the backdrop of shifting experiences of day-to-day life and fragmenting tendencies of modern institutions (Giddens 1984). The basis for such a general approach to theory of social identity can already be found half a century earlier in the work of the American philosopher George Herbert Mead (1934) in his discussion of selfhood. He emphasizes reflexivity of the self as it is created in the process of social interaction and particularly "symbolic interaction" (Mead 1934; Jenkins 1996). The very self-reflexive and interactive character of the Jewish identities of the representatives of the third generation of Jews in Poland will be discussed further.

A number of theorists and researchers, unsatisfied with the claims of social constructionism, challenged the fear of essentialism even further through attempts to examine the reasons why essentialist identity claims do not cease to exist (Calhoun 1995; Cerulo 1997; Gil-White 1999; Weinreich et al. 2003). I shall discuss this issue later on in light of the results of this study.

Another significant theoretical contribution ought to be mentioned here, namely the growing emphasis put on the notion of collective identity (and identification), as well as on multiple, often contradictory identities (Ashmore et al. 2004; Holland et al. 2001). Two disparate pictures of the relationship between culture and identity can be discerned in the ongoing debate on the subject. The first one is known as the culturalist approach, and is related to the broader essentialist perspective. The culturalists view individuals as bearers of culture in that the latter's principles determine how individuals behave. This view of identity is contrasted with the constructivist approach, where identities are lived in and through activity, as they develop in social practice. In the constructivist view, people are not just products of culture and not just respondents to the situation but appropriators of cultural artifacts that they themselves and others produce (Holland et al. 2001).

Along with the belief that individuals are free to choose their identity, to freely decide who they are going to be and where they are going to belong, there exists the assumption that for each person there exists a set of choices they are most likely to make. There is a sense of sociability, which manipulates, albeit to a degree, a person's sense of individuality. In other words, individuals may be "free within a context," but they are not "free of context" (Tamir 1996, 47). On the one hand, culture no longer fully controls who we are, but on the other hand, it is culture precisely that conditions how we choose who to be. The specific time-spatial conditions of identity construction processes described in this study must once again be emphasized. This will also be done by the participants themselves in their own narratives, which will be analyzed further.

Hall mentions that however fluid identity can be, or however uprooted, it nevertheless seeks a source of stability and rootedness (though they may never be found) (Burszta 2004). In this sense, not only are we conditioned by culture but we actually long for some of its elements, such as tradition or community. As pointed out by Bauman, "identity sprouts on the graveyard of communities, but flourishes thanks to its promise to resurrect the dead" (Bauman 2001, 481). At the risk of oversimplifying, Jewish identity in the third generation is being constructed in Poland on the graveyard of the Polish Jewish community as it was known before the war. But the hope to "resurrect the dead" is part and parcel of the individual identity narratives, whether explicit or implicit.

Community and tradition are considered important elements in the contemporary debate on identity (Burszta 2004). However, the theory of detraditionalization claims that tradition today is not as big a factor as it used to be in the construction of identity at the individual and at the collective level. Detraditionalists speak of a fading of traditions in that people have ceased to believe that they are part of a greater whole (Giddens 1991; Piccone 1992). This is accompanied by the belief that one can exist outside society. In its extreme version, then, the notion of detraditionalization is not entirely believable. The alternative approach is one that acknowledges the coexistence of tradition and detradition-alization. Here, detraditionalization is a process that undoubtedly exists, but it happens along opposite processes of building traditions and of reconstructing traditional forms of living (see Heelas et al. 1996). It is not that chaos, fluidity, and uncertainty have replaced culture and tradition, but rather that they all exist simultaneously and condition one another (Burszta 2004).

Rather than discredit the validity of identity in social research, rendering it too ambiguous and thus devoid of analytical import (as some analysts have suggested; e.g., Brubaker and Cooper 2000), my study insists on appreciating the constructed nature of identity. More specifically, I support the view that sees identity as constructed and as a process of self-understanding (Horenczyk and Bekerman 1999). This approach can be identified as the narrative approach, and it involves appreciating the construction of identity as a phenomenon of a narrative nature (Bakhtin 1984; Carr 1986; Gergen 1994; Giddens 1991; MacIntyre 1981; Taylor 1989). Although the philosophical inspirations of the narrative approach can be associated (among other theories) with Martin Heidegger's existential ontology and Edmund Husserl's phenomenology (Heidegger 1927; Husserl 1970), it must be mentioned that the narrative approach remains closely linked to discourse theory (Rosner 2003). To view identities as discursively constructed is an alternative to the reifying essentialist conceptions of identity (Fraser 1992). To appraise existing forms of discourse is to evaluate patterns of cultural life, and it is part and parcel of the broader constructionist approach (Burr 1995; Gergen 1994). Narrative is the structure of understanding, within which life events are contained, and it is dynamic and self-reflexive (MacIntyre 1981; see also Rosner 2003). In this sense, identity is a process through which people construct a personal narrative, which allows them to make sense of their lives (Giddens 1991). And it is the objective of the present study to try to make sense of the identities of the third post-Holocaust generation of Jews living in Poland through an analysis of their individual narratives.

In this study, I support the general philosophical assumptions, the "what" and the "how" (ontology and epistemology), which guide the work on both narrative and discourse in social sciences. Consequently, I recognize that discourse extends beyond linguistic expression and that it also pertains to socially situated practices (Gee 1992), to existing social discourses, which fashion the "self" (Foucault 1973; Gergen 1992; Hall 1996), to dialogical interaction being conditioned by discursive domains (Bakhtin 1981; Potter and Whetherell 1987), and to "interpretative repertoires" (Nairn and McCreanor 1991; Wetherell and Potter 1992). For the present study, I operate within a broad understanding of identity as a process whereby individuals organize their relationships with the world, in every sense of the word. And if such an identity is continuously discursively constructed against day-to-day experiences, then we may argue that in young Polish Jews, we have a case of an exceptionally dynamic and self-reflexive process of narrative construction of identity, which fulfills itself in discussion. What defines the nature of their identities are the individual inner discussions, the relentless passionate discussions with one another, and the challenging, invigorating discussions with the outside world.

ETHNICITY

OUR INTEREST IN THE dialectic of the two contrasting approaches to personal identity extends to the discussion of ethnicity as one of the most debated domains of identity. Thus, the juxtapositions of choice and determinism, of the given and the constructed, or of essence and variation will also serve as useful tools for understanding the complexities involved in defining ethnic identity. This is not to say that I will try to define Jewishness in contemporary Poland in terms of ethnicity but rather to appreciate that certain ethnic identity theories and concepts very much help inform the Jewish identity experience as narrated by our participants.

Numerous theories of ethnic identity have made careers in the second half of the twentieth century. Social anthropologist Fredrik Barth (1969) defines ethnic groups as units of ascription, with social boundaries ensuring the persistence of the group, while being permeable and allowing across-group transactions. According to Barth, it is ethnic boundaries that define a group. The strongest claim here is that ethnic groups are rational associations of self-interested actors, who choose rationally to ascribe themselves to a given group (Barth 1969; see also Gil-White 1999). Henri Tajfel's (1981) acclaimed social identity theory asserts that assignment to a group is accompanied by the assumption of its higher value, which results in an enhanced collective self-esteem (see also Liebkind 1992). Here, ethnic identity is seen as a component of an individual's social identity (see also Phinney 2003). A similar approach can be found in Donald Horowitz's (1985) social-psychological approach, where some of the factors that define an ethnic group are collective stereotypes, myths of kinship, and group honor.

One of the most operative definitions of ethnic identity nowadays is one proposed by Jean S. Phinney (2003), who describes ethnic identity as "a dynamic, multidimensional construct that refers to one's identity, or sense of self as a member of an ethnic group" (Phinney 2003, 63). Phinney supports Smith's (1998) definition in saying that ethnic identity assumes the existence of common ancestry, shared culture, language, race, or place. Significantly, Phinney (2003) describes ethnic identity as a dynamic construct, which involves an individual pursuit of an understanding of one's self and ethnic background.

Ethnic identity has also been analyzed within the framework of acculturation. Two different approaches can be distinguished here. The first one is the linear approach, where ethnic identity is conceptualized against a range from strong ethnic ties to strong mainstream ties. This model assumes that strong ethnic identity is impossible among people involved in the mainstream society (Gordon 1964). In contrast, the bipolar model of ethnic identity allows for identification with both the ethnic group and the mainstream society, where both identifications are meaningful and both or either can be strong (Berry 1990; Horenczyk and Ben-Shalom 2006).

One of the major analytical frameworks in the debate on ethnic identity stems from the continuing controversy between primordialism and circumstantialism. With regard to the concept of identity, we contrasted the essentialist perspective with the social-constructionist and postmodern perspectives as different ontological and epistemological-methodological approaches. In the context of ethnicity, the two major discursive approaches are represented by primordialism and circumstantialism. I will show just how relevant the controversy proves to be in the contemporary Jewish identity debate.

The introduction of the concept of primordialism into social studies is associated with sociologist Edward Shils (1957). He spoke of "ineffable significance," which is attributed to the "tie of blood" (Shils 1957), yet his work contained little further discussion of the notion of primordialism. Primordial traits were described more extensively by the prominent American social anthropologist Clifford Geertz (1963). He defined them in terms of "givens" of social existence, which possess an "ineffable, overpowering coerciveness" and are compelling, determinist, involuntary, and inborn (Geertz 1963). Primary kinship is associated with common biological descent, race, language, region, and religion (Geertz 1963; see also McKay 1982). Hence, the basic assumption of primordialism is that individuals are born as involuntary members of a given ethnic community. Therefore, belonging is secured by birth (or blood). One cannot choose to belong; ethnicity is a fixed role ascribed to a passive individual. In this view, to be a Jew is to be born into a Jewish family, to have a Jewish blood link, and to possess the irrevocable "racial" trait. The circumstantialist perspective on the other hand (which is also called constructivist, mobilizationist, situationalist, or instrumentalist) emphasizes the socially constructed nature of ethnicity and interprets ethnic mobilization in terms of indications of concrete interests, whether political, social, or economic. This view acknowledges the possibility of changing ethnic identifications as well as of new ethnicities arising (Gil-White 1999). In the most extreme scenario, circumstantialists see ethnicity and the mobilization of ethnic symbols as attempts at accessing social, political, or economic resources. It is all about interests and strategy. Individuals are seen as rational actors (see also Barth 1969).

Both primordialism and circumstantialism present certain conceptual limitations. The problem with the circumstantialist model is that naturally social and political interests are not the sole objects of people's struggles, and it seems overstated to try to explain the existence of ethnicities in this way. In other words, it is fair to say that ethnic groups may have interests, but it does not necessarily imply that we ought to define them *in terms* of those interests (Epstein 1978; McKay 1982). On the other hand, the problem with the primordialist model is that it does not allow for the possibility of change or of dynamic characteristics of ethnic collectivities. Moreover, primordialists seem to talk about ethnic groups as if they existed in a social, political, and economic vacuum, as if there were no reasons for ethnic identification except that inborn "inner urge" (McKay 1982) or even a "must." Finally, there is a high degree of insiderism in primordial thinking, which is represented in the assumption that we cannot learn anything about other people unless we actually *are them*.

Anthony D. Smith (1998) discusses both approaches in the controversy, providing an alternative in the form of a combination of the two. He describes the primordial element as a given of human existence and the situational (circumstantial) element as a perspective for seeing ethnicity as a tool for determining attitudes and perceptions of belonging to a group. Smith's alternative combines social constructionism with essentialist or primordialist arguments, as he explains ethnicity in terms of a kind of primordial continuity (a preexisting collective identity and community), which is necessarily supported by conscious manipulation in the form of ideology. It is the fictive descent, attachment to territory, shared memories and myths, symbolic-cultural attributes, historical memories, religion, language, customs, and color that are endowed with significance by a group of individuals and thus account for ethnic identification (Cerulo 1997; Smith 1998).

According to primordial theories of ethnocultural groups or of nations, the latter already existed before the modern period (Hastings 1997). Smith's (2001) approach in the form of ethnosymbolism is again some form of moderate primordialism. He compares nations to artichokes, which have a lot of superficial leaves, but also have a heart, which always remains as "the essence" (Smith 2001). Contrary to the previously mentioned theories, the modernists see ethnocultural groups or nations as distinctly modern inventions, generated by capitalism (Gellner 1983) or even by imagination, where they nevertheless remain powerful (Anderson 1965). According to modernists, then, ethnicity is a modern phenomenon closely related to processes of change. In this view, ethnic ties are constantly redefined in light of changing social and political conditions (Gil-White 1999).

Various theories of ethnicity, among them primordialism and circumstantialism, attempt to explain ethnic affiliations and identities. However, they also provide a discursive framework which offers tools for analyzing people's own accounts of ethnic sentiments. A good example of a theoretical approach that emphasizes discourse is that of Weinreich et al. (2003). They categorized people's discourse on ethnicity along the two dimensions—primordialist and situationalist. Their approach addresses the question of why primordialist sentiments continue to be present in people's discourses and how this basic human propensity becomes challenged to allow situationalist or circumstantialist perspectives (Weinreich et al. 2003). The concept of ethnic identity can therefore serve as a means of asserting oneself in the face of threats to one's identity (Weinreich 1983). This notion proves to be central in the present study and will be analyzed in depth in the further sections of the book.

Certain attempts have been made to avoid automatic dichotomization of the primordialist and circumstantialist perspectives by appreciating their mutually complementary theoretical input and/or by focusing on their role as analytical categories of a discursive nature (Gil-White 1999; Liebkind 1992; McKay 1982). It must be appreciated that the theories of primordialism and of circumstantialism lend hand to the discursive repertoire of human beings, as they make references to ethnic commitments, blood ties, ancestry, or common fate.

As indicated earlier, although primordialist and circumstantialist views are usually discussed as alternative theories of ethnicity and ethnic identification (and as such they evoke a lot of criticism), I am interested in analyzing the ways in which the two approaches are expressed (explicitly and implicitly) in people's accounts of their Jewishness and of Jewish affiliations. Primordialist and circumstantialist concepts will prove central in our efforts to make sense of the identity narratives of the representatives of the third post-Holocaust generation of Jews in Poland.

JEWISH IDENTITY

THE QUESTION OF JEWISH identity is a central one in this study, and perhaps it is one that evades all unambiguous definitions. One wonders whether the concept of identity is any more puzzling than the notion of Jewish. It is perhaps all the more poignant in our specific context just how far from self-evident the notions of "Jewish" and "identity" are. Consequently, the best way to proceed is to present a selection of theoretical approaches to the idea of Jewish identity and to confront them with our results in the following chapters.

It is perhaps fair to say that before the mid-nineteenth century, debates on Jewish identity, if at all present among Jews or non-Jews, were confined to the private sphere. With the advent of the Haskalah—the Jewish Enlightenment, emancipation, the French Revolution, and the social and technological-industrial revolutions, the definitions of the Jewish collective and of Jewish identity were put into question and appear to remain "in question" until this day. Religious reform in Judaism only fostered the debate on Jewishness, as did antisemitism, communism, and the Shoah.

A comprehensive approach to Jewish identity was offered by Israeli sociologist Eliezer Ben-Rafael (2002). He suggests that we analyze Jewish identity as a particular case of collective identity. With the assumption that collective identity cannot necessarily be defined in terms of a single, consistent essence, Ben-Rafael distinguishes three different "phases" in discussing collective identity. The first one is concerned with the way in which people describe their link and their obligations to a particular collective. The second "phase" pertains to the way people describe the cultural, social, normative, religious, historical, or linguistic singularity of the given collective. The third aspect relates to the way the individuals perceive the collective in relation to "others" (Ben-Rafael 2002). Ben-Rafael goes on to say that before the modern era, Jewish identity could be characterized as a caste identity, with a shared and relatively unquestioned connection to God, Torah, the Jewish

People, and the Land of Israel. Alongside the singularity of the Jewish People, there existed a universal accent in that the Jews had a crucial role in achieving an overall supreme purpose for the benefit of all (Ben-Rafael 2002). Smith's (1987) sociological definition speaks of caste as numerous social practices that merge discourse (language, ideas, and symbols) with action (activities, behavioral patterns, environmental and institutional features, etc.). These practices are endowed with religious legitimacy, which derives from the perception of "purity." It is for purity's sake that contact with "others" is limited or nonexistent. This, however, is paired by the collective's self-perception as part of a larger system, where the ideas of supreme purpose and transcendental meaning come to play. As such, Jews were a caste within the societies they lived among. A caste of pariahs or inferiors in the eyes of the "others" but a superior caste in their own perception (Ben-Rafael 2002).

Ben-Rafael (2002) describes how during the nineteenth century and due to the modernization processes, the relationship between Jews and non-Jews changed radically, as did the Jews' own approach to their Jewishness. On the one hand, the Jews had to respond to the cultural-national and the technological-industrial revolutions in Europe, and on the other hand, they were faced with their own internal dilemmas. The first internal dilemma stemmed from the question of whether Jews could be defined as a cultural or social community rather than a primarily religious one. The second question regarded the God of Israel and the Hebrew Bible—if the reality was going to be primarily secular, what would happen to the perceived singularity of the Jewish People? Would the Jews now be a culture, a history, or perhaps a shared fate? The third dilemma was related to the Land of Israel—should it still represent an actual eternal and future homeland of the Jews, or should it be perceived as a metaphor (Ben-Rafael 2002)? The different approaches to the previously mentioned dilemmas were represented in the different denominations of Judaism and Jewish social movements which emerged with Modernity and in the era(s) that followed.

My analysis remains sensitive to the two approaches to identity in general, which reflect two different approaches to Jewish identity in particular. The first approach maintains that identity or Jewish identity is a fixed, stable entity, which exists above time and space. The other sees identity as a process conditioned by time and space and by circumstances; one that realizes itself in constantly responding to circumstances. For example, British social anthropologist Jonathan Webber (1994) suggests that we talk about Jewish identities in the plural and that we view them as constructs in response to circumstances.

Along the lines of the postmodern theories of identity mentioned earlier (e.g. Bauman 2001; Foucault 1973; Gergen 1992; Giddens 1991; Hall 1992; Lifton 1993), Michael Krausz (1993) offers an interesting typology, where he juxtaposes two conceptions of Jewish identity. The first one stems from an essentialist understanding of human nature. According to this view, a person's identity is embodied in a stable essence which is a-historical and a-social; therefore, one simply is a Jew or is not. In other words, this approach presumes that there are fixed conditions for "a thing" to be that thing (Krausz 1993). Krausz (1993) calls this type of Jewish identity "Jewishness by descent." Such a position naturally evokes the notion of primordialism as well as fixed identity theories, both of which were discussed earlier. "Jewishness by descent" is contrasted with "Jewishness by assent." The concept of "Jewishness by assent" asserts that there is no essence to the Jewish people, there are only Jewish positions, and Jewishness is a set of characteristics, in which certain people are cast or which are ascribed to them—by themselves and by others (Krausz 1993).

Again, although a Jew by descent is born Jewish and never ceases to be Jewish, Jewishness by assent involves identification with a historical group. It involves situating oneself in one's present and in a historically projectable discursive situation. Krausz carefully adds that he does not claim that any discourse can be privileged as the one that captures the singularly right construal of Jewish identity. In other words, there is no single fact of the matter as to what Jewishness is (Krausz 1993, 273).

A similar theoretical exposition of Jewish identity based on the general juxtaposition of the more traditional understanding of identity and of the more critical one is that of Berel Lang (1993). He too offers an interpretation based on antinomies. He first distinguishes between Jewish identity as "a matter of fact" and Jewish identity as "a matter of choice." Jewish identity as a matter of fact is understood to be determined on the basis of objective criteria to which the person whose identity is at issue has no privileged access. On the other hand, Jewish identity as a matter of choice is understood to be made by the person whose identity is in question (Lang 1993). Lang (1993) suggests that historically speaking, the conditions of Jewish identity have been defined in objective terms—one had to be born from a Jewish mother. This is a perception of Jewish identity as determined and permanent, not something that can be renounced. It is then a function of the individual's historical and social past, and it is particularistic and exclusionary. In other words, it is primordial—inherent, inborn, given, and inscribed "in blood," if you like.

When perceived in terms of choice, however, Jewish identity involves more than just the physical, "biological" fact and more than just identification by others—it involves a self-definition, affirmation, and/or choice. This also assumes the freedom to dissent or to change. In such a view, Jewish identity is a function of the individual's immediate present (including present interpretation of his historical and social past). Although history is important to one's identity, for the past to have a meaning, an individual always has to confirm, deny, or in some way actively respond to it (Lang 1993). In other words, Jewish identity is constructed in response to circumstances, in response to the past and to the present alike.

It may be trivial to say, once again, that there is no one satisfying all-encompassing definition of Jewish identity. Who the Jews are or who a Jew is are questions which both Jews and non-Jews have repeatedly failed to answer in an authoritative way (Selzer 1968). We can find numerous definitions of who the Jews are, and not only different Jews, but also non-Jews propose disparate definitions.

Some have tried to create a definition on the basis of who a Jew is *not*. In his controversial approach, Jean-Paul Sartre (1948) offered an analysis of Jewish identity as constructed through the principle of difference in relation to the dominant cultural identity of non-Jews. Although the French philosopher's approach was met with much criticism for offering a negative and highly reductionist definition of Jewishness, his basic principle is that of Jewish identity being a relational and a dynamic phenomenon, and as such it deserves our attention (Charmé 1998).

Alongside Sartre's ideas, Stuart Charmé (2000) discusses the difference between essentialist and existentialist understandings of Jewish identity. The essentialist approach maintains that there is an essential, unalterable content to Jewish identity which renders it authentic, whereas the existential approach appreciates the historical and dynamic nature of identity and grants Jewish identity the possibility of being constantly questioned and negotiated in response to circumstances (Charmé 2000).

Anthony Smith (1992) maintains that the image of the Jewish people nowadays is that of an identity in transition. He explains that Jews are not merely a religious group, nor are they a nation per se, but rather they constitute a resilient "demotic ethnie," where a central role is played by ethnic memory (Smith 1992).

In my study, I remain sensitive to different conceptualizations of Jewish identity. At the same time, I am aware of the fact that new phenomena continue to emerge, which call for a reassessment of the existing range of conceptual tools for analyzing the construction of Jewish identities. In the discussion and conclusions section, I shall address some of the ways in which the particular Jewish identity stories presented in this study may challenge existing analytical categories. In light of the narratives of the representatives of the third post-Holocaust generation of Jews in Poland, I will present an alternative approach to the dichotomy between primordialism and circumstantialism, which emphasizes their uniquely interdependent nature.

CONVERSION

THE CONCEPT OF CONVERSION is generally discussed in the context of religion. In this study, I resort also to its broader understanding as a process of personal transformation, that is, not necessarily as a merely religious phenomenon (Lamb and Bryant 1999). It should be noted that the participants in this study are people who undergo processes of transformation, and whether they join a religious conversion group or not, they carry stories of identities in transition. Notably, all of the participants have Jewish roots, which—if in fact they decide to formally convert—nevertheless makes them a "special" category of converts. In addition, the sole option of undergoing the ritual of conversion is ever-present in the discourse of today's Polish Jews and thus remains a key reference in the formation of individual narratives.

Sociological and psychological literature distinguishes between various types of conversion, motives for conversion, and motifs in conversion narratives. It also talks about a number of subsequent stages in the conversion process (Rambo 1993). Types of such religious transition identified by Lewis R. Rambo (1993) are defined as follows: apostasy (or defection)—rejection of a previous tradition; intensification—deepening or "revitalizing" of an existing commitment; affiliation—full involvement with a community one had minimal or no involvement with; institutional transition—choosing one community over another within a major tradition; or tradition transition—moving from one major tradition to another (Rambo 1993). In my study, these terms serve as conceptual instruments used to understand and interpret the narratives of people giving accounts of their identity transition.

Analyzing the processes of conversion also provides us with conceptual tools for understanding the narratives of personal transformation. Rambo and Farhadian's (1999) model mentions seven stages: (1) context—the environment, where (2) crisis occurs and triggers a (3) quest, that is, seeking new ways in life, which eventually leads to an (4) encounter with an advocate of the alternative "way." Thus, (5) interaction is established, which fosters (6) commitment and leads to (7) consequences, which may facilitate or hinder converting. It is worth noting that the previously mentioned model is not necessarily sequential, and that the conversion it speaks of is understood first and foremost as an official, ritualistic entry into a new religious system.

The previously mentioned stage model can be evaluated against another perspective, which is essentially a narrative approach, analyzing different themes or "motifs" within the conversion narrative. Psychologists of religion Lofland and Skonovd (1981) differentiate between six kinds of motifs: intellectual, with the primacy of knowledge of a system over social contact; mystical, where a sudden insight or paranormal experience occurs; experimental, which is realized in "trying out" the system; affectional, that is, being loved and nurtured by the group and its leaders; revivalist, that is, being aroused within a crowd by means of powerful music, preaching, and so on; and coercive, which may involve brainwashing, psychological programming, or even torture. Aware of the many limitations of such categories, I use some of them in analyzing the stories of personal transformations, as articulated in the words of the participants.

In the case of conversion to Judaism, questions arise of both religious as well as ethnic boundaries. The nature of conversion carries direct relevance to the question of identity of the Jewish collective (Sagi and Zohar 1994). Converting to Judaism means becoming Jewish not only in the sense of a religious conviction but also in the sense of peoplehood. It is religion, however, which has to be embraced to gain access to the Jewish people (Mariner 1999). Rabbinic literature engages in a discussion of the relationship between the motives for conversion and the process of converting per se (for an extensive analysis, see Sagi and Zohar 1994). As indicated by Mariner (1999) in his socio-historical review of conversion to Judaism, "a born Jew may choose to identify through peoplehood or culture, the proselyte may only enter through the door of religion" (Mariner 1999, 99). The complex nature of conversion to Judaism is discussed in this study as one of the frameworks for "narrating identity." Again, the critical remark here is that the laws and the conduct of religious conversion reflect the collective vision of belonging and of cultural identity as constructed from the inside perspective. They demarcate cultural boundaries.

As controversial as conversion to Judaism proves to be in reality, inasmuch as it raises major questions with regard to authenticity, it remains crucial within the discourse pertinent to contemporary debates on Jewish identity and Jewish culture. A single reference to conversion to Judaism often proves indicative of a specific understanding of Jewish culture and identity, of boundaries of Jewish identity, and of the often-confusing notion of (Jewish) authenticity.

In the following paragraphs, I provide a brief overview of different approaches to the notion of authenticity, which have influenced contemporary discourse of identity.

AUTHENTICITY

THE NOTION OF AUTHENTICITY has been present in philosophy and sociology for many decades. However, only in the past thirty years has it become practically immanent to the discourse of identity, especially in the debate on the construction of the "modern self." My perspective on authenticity is a socio-anthropological one, though I am also interested in authenticity's discursive potential in identity narratives.

Tracing the history of the notion of authenticity would involve looking into nearly all theories of identity and ethnicity, including those which do not mention authenticity in a direct manner. It would also involve giving an account of numerous chapters in history of philosophy. Allow me to bring up only a few selected theories.

Philosophers first found themselves interested in the idea of authenticity in the general ethical perspective, as it emerged on the basis of the eighteenth century's individualism. We can trace the idea from "disengaged rationalism" of René Descartes (1911) with its "think for yourself" formula, through the political individualism of John Locke (1997) with its primacy of free will over social obligations, to what Jean-Jacques Rousseau (1973) would call *le sentiment de l'éxistence*—moral contact with oneself and self-inwardness versus the outside world. Somewhere at the crossroads of these and similar postulates, Johann Gottfried Herder (2002) would claim that every man has his own measure, his own way of being human, and his own obligation to be "faithful" to himself. And that, roughly, became the ethical ideal inherited by Modernity. In *Being and Time*, Heidegger (1927) talks of two modes of "being": the inauthentic and the authentic, where the latter involves a commitment to oneself, distinguishing between one's own needs and feelings for others, and questioning that which is established and fixed.

Sartre (1948) addressed the issue of authenticity from an existentialist point of view. What characterizes "existential authenticity" according to the French philosopher is "ontological insecurity," transcending all certainties, fixed roles, and established categories. What Charles

Taylor (1989) will later call *horizons of meaning*, in a claim that the idea of authenticity assumes the existence of external meanings and values, Sartre called the *other* or *otherness*, with its reverse movement of passing, with its "uncivilized vulgarity," its fluctuating, excluded, and uprooted identity (Sartre 1948; see also Charmé 2000).

Although Modernity may have aspired to be the era of the pursuit of authenticity, it seems fair to say that postmodernity brought along a climate of inauthenticity (Erickson 1995). It is the lack of authenticity that seems to be of more interest to the postmodern observer. Rebecca Erickson (1995) offers a reconceptualization of authenticity in terms of a trans-situational system of values, in a way that allows for inconsistency within the self, not rendering it inauthentic. This approach emphasizes the role of context and relationships, where the necessary diversity involved in being true to the self in context and true to the self in relationship is nevertheless axiologically structured (Erickson 1995).

The question of authenticity proves curiously poignant within the debate on contemporary Jewish identity. Charmé (2000) distinguishes between what he describes as essentialist authenticity and existential authenticity. He analyzes the question of an "authentic Jewish identity," pointing out two distinct qualities: the essentialist reference to a "Jewish content" and the existential quality of a personal identity. In other words, the latter would involve asking about the authenticity of the Jewish qualifier of one's self, whereas the previous asks about one's own sense of authenticity (Charmé 2000).

Another take on authenticity was offered by Avi Sagi (2002), who argues that the discourse of authentic identity in the constructionist framework involves an abandonment of notions of "true Jewishness" as well as of hierarchies of Jewishness according to degree of authenticity. Sagi goes on to say that constructivist discourse of identity can be rendered authentic only if it remains pluralist. In other words, it ought to grant the value of authenticity to all alternative constructions of Jewishness (Sagi 2002).

Contemporary Poland, with its much debated "revival" of Jewish culture, in the form of Jewish culture festivals and other artistic enterprises, as well as its post-transition revitalization of the local Jewish community, has become a popular "target" of questions about authenticity. There has been a very significant non-Jewish creative input in the representations of Jewish culture in Poland since the late 1980s.

Moreover, the majority of the "consumers" of those representations have also been non-Jews. All this provokes much discussion surrounding the authenticity of the so-called "Jewish renaissance."

My interest within the framework of this study is in authenticity as a major factor in the construction of Jewish identities. I will focus on the rhetoric of authenticity in the personal narratives and in the ongoing debate on the "revival" of Jewishness in Poland, where accusations of inauthenticity are multiple. It must be appreciated that the identities of the third post-Holocaust generation of Jews are constructed in Poland alongside a no less intriguing process of construction of what Ruth Ellen Gruber called "new authenticities" (Gruber 2009). Even if the process of "Jewish revival" in Poland can be associated with drawing on imagined and sometimes stereotypical notions of Judaism, it has nevertheless managed to produce what Gruber calls "real imaginary spaces," which now have a certain undeniable reality (Gruber 2002). And it is in this new reality that Jewish life in Poland happens.

In this study, I trace different responses to the question of authenticity which transpire in particular contexts. The case of young Jews in Poland reveals a number of different dimensions of the rhetoric of authenticity, which reflect the complexities involved in being Jewish in Poland as well as being recognized as Jewish by multiple "others."

* * *

The previously mentioned theoretical frameworks provide a firmer footing for our research question (Creswell 2003). Let me restate then that this study undertakes to portray the ways in which the representatives of the third post-Holocaust generation of Jews in contemporary Poland narrate their experience of embracing Jewishness. I look at how their narratives convey the story of the discovery of Jewish ancestry, of the processes of self-defining, and of making references to different domains of meaning. Furthermore, I examine the discursive patterns, which emerge in the participants' attempts to "make sense of" their "condition." Finally, I remain alert to the theoretical frameworks of identity, ethnicity, conversion, and authenticity as I analyze the personal accounts of involvement in Jewishness, of self-understanding, of locating oneself within the particular socio-cultural circumstance, and of creating models of self-authentication.

METHOD

Participants

I CONDUCTED FIFTY INTERVIEWS with young adults born between the 1970s and the early 1990s. The interviews were conducted in person, except one, which was conducted online using an instant messaging program. Thirty-nine interviews were audio recorded, and ten were recorded on video. The sample includes mostly people who learned about their Jewish ancestry in their teens. Six of the interviewees maintain that they already knew about Jewish roots in their family early in childhood. They too, however, began the process of pursuing a Jewish affiliation only in their teens. The sample was chosen from among people between the ages of eighteen and thirty-five years, and it includes people who have a Jewish parent or grandparent. Five of the interviewees were younger than twenty years, eight were older than thirty years, and thirty-seven were in their twenties. They included thirty-one women and nineteen men. Fourteen participants have a Jewish mother, nineteen have a Jewish father, twelve have a Jewish grandfather, one has both a Jewish mother and a Jewish father, and five have an unclear "roots situation," that is, they live in the conviction that their mothers are Jewish, although they are currently unable to prove it. Thirty participants are from Warsaw, eight are from Wroclaw, and the remaining twelve come from various cities, including Poznan, Lodz, and Krakow. I refrain from disclosing more specifically which towns particular interviewees come from in order not to jeopardize their anonymity. Three participants were living in Israel at the time of the interview, and two of them have since returned to Poland. One of my participants moved to Israel since the interview, but continues to be actively involved in Jewish life in Poland.

At the time of the interview, ten of my interviewees identified as observant Modern Orthodox, or were considering becoming more observant. The remaining forty identified as "not religious," though many among them endorse some elements of Jewish tradition. Forty out of fifty participants have been baptized.

The participants are individuals who began seeking a form of Jewish affiliation in their teens, that is in the 1990s and the 2000s, and most of them are formally or informally affiliated with the Polish Union of Jewish Students or—as it is known since 2007—the Polish Jewish Youth Organization (ŻOOM). The organization is estimated to have approximately 400 members. The Krakow-based participants are mostly members of the Krakow-based Jewish association known as *Czulent* and/or with the Krakow JCC, also estimated to have approximately 400 members. All the participants represent the Polish middle class, and all of them either have or intend to acquire a college education. Thirty-one of the participants who have obtained a college degree or were enrolled in a degree program are students or graduates in the field of humanities. More than half of the participants are today in one way or another professionally involved in the Jewish organizational network, in Jewish culture, or in Jewish studies, whereas all of them are generally informally involved in Jewish communal life and in secular and/or religious communal activities.

Procedure

THIS STUDY IS CONCERNED with narratives of identity—with the ways in which people interpret their worlds and with what they say their worlds are like (Bogdan and Taylor 1975; Bruner 1990; Maykut and Morehouse 1994). Therefore, I resorted to interviewing as the most operative method in the type of research, which aims at an understanding of how people manage to understand themselves. I stress the importance of approaching phenomena as they appear in the worlds, in the perspectives, and in the language of the persons under study (Kotarba and Fontana 1984; Marcus and Fischer 1986). At the same time, I appreciate that, as pointed out by Bruner (1990), the realities people construct are "social realities, negotiated with others" and "distributed between them" (Bruner 1990, 105–106).

Although I used the conversational, open-ended form of interviewing, I formulated some questions aimed at acquiring certain sets of information about each of the participants. I prefer to call this kind of interviewing "relatively unstructured" rather than semi-structured, as no actual structure can be discerned neither in the organization nor in the conduct of the interviews. Furthermore, I did not have a list of general questions but only a list of topics to encourage during the interview. The ideas I had in mind and wanted to provoke my interviewees to address were the product of participant observation and previous conversations with the representatives of the third generation. Although I was interested in discussing particular trajectories in the lives of the participants, I did not use a prearranged series of questions, which would resemble a structure.

I used snowball sampling, which involved asking the persons I already decided I wanted to interview (mostly acquaintances of mine) for further contacts (mostly acquaintances of theirs). The interviews took place between 2001 and 2011 in Warsaw, Wroclaw, Krakow, and Jerusalem. They were conducted in informal settings in a relaxed atmosphere (often accompanied by drinks and snacks). Forty interviews were in-depth audio interviews, which lasted between 1.5 and 3 hours. The remaining ten were shorter video interviews, which lasted between 30 and 60 minutes. All interviews were in Polish. The forty participants interviewed on audio were assured of the confidentiality of the research. The ten video interviews were not anonymous. However, in this book, the names of all interviewees have been changed.

My interviews focused on diverse experiences of the introduction to the knowledge of one's Jewish ancestry as well as the subsequent decision to pursue a form of Jewish affiliation. I tried to trace the participants' involvement in communal life and in public cultural ventures. At the same time, I asked about changes in their social networks, their relationships with friends and family, and their participation in Jewish and non-Jewish social circles. The interviews aimed at an understanding of the individuals' self-image in relation to Jewishness and Polishness and of their attitude toward other Jews, religious observance, the Shoah, antisemitism, and the State of Israel. I asked about their attitude to conversion to Judaism and about reasons for and consequences of converting. I sought to grasp how the participants see themselves in relation to contemporary Polish society, the Polish Jewish community, and—finally—the international Jewish community. The interviews also put an emphasis on the individuals' plans, including the criteria of choosing a partner in life, organizing a home, and raising potential children, as well as the individual ways of negotiating ("authentic") modes of Jewish existence.

ANALYSIS

ONCE METICULOUSLY TRANSCRIBED, THE interviews provided the basis for my analysis. The latter focused on uncovering the patterns involved in the activity of locating oneself in the cultural landscape through the telling of one's story, through evaluative statements about the past, the present, and the future. I paid attention to how people talk about themselves in terms of time, in terms of space, and in terms of values.

I sought to maintain a perspectival view (Maykut and Morehouse 1994) in trying to give an account of the personal stories of my interviewees. The interviews provided a means of collecting stories as they are recollected by the participants. Such self-narratives transmit individual and cultural meanings (Lieblich et al. 1998). My inquiry began with recollections of the different types of introduction to Jewish ancestry experienced by the participants. During the interviews, I encouraged stories of the development of particular Jewish affiliations. This gave me insight into the individual ways of expressing ideas about identity and its constructive factors. I could thus analyze the patterns emerging in the activity of narrating identity.

Stories reveal individual ways of experiencing reality and allow the researcher to access people's identity (Lieblich et al. 1998). In fact, some theorists have come to believe that personal narratives *are* people's identities (e.g. Bruner 1990; Gergen 1994). Be that as it may, self-narratives must be acknowledged as the means by which identities are fashioned (Rosenwald and Ochberg 1992). The story helps access not only an individual's identity but also the culture the given person participates in. In pursuing narrative analysis, I strove to reconcile three voices: (1) the voice of the narrator, (2) the theoretical framework as a source of tools for interpretation, and (3) the reflexive monitoring of the act of reading and interpreting (Lieblich et al. 1998).

Transition has been pointed out as one of the peculiar breaking points, highlighted and endorsed with meaning by the narrators of life stories (McAdams et al. 2001). My concrete narrators are people who undoubtedly experienced major transition in their lives, and the interviews have shown how they narrate that experience. The analysis of personal accounts consists of interpreting interpretations, as my narrator him or herself already provides the primary interpretation. Hence, the analysis accounts for creating a "meta-story" (Riessman, 1993).

During the process of analysis, hypotheses, which refined further reading, and concepts, which continued to inform it, were generated. This generated a growing circle of understanding, as constructed along the principles of grounded theory (Charmaz 1995; Lieblich et al. 1998). The analysis of the qualitative data involved data-driven inductive hypothesis generation, where concepts and their interrelationships were subsequently abstracted from the data (Kelle 1995; Punch 1998). I used coding in the form of labeling chunks of data, which provided the basis for identifying patterns. This was followed by the process of developing descriptive and inferential codes. The activity of coding was carried out along the tenets of grounded theory (Charmaz 1995; Glaser 1978; Punch 1998; Strauss and Corbin 1994). It involved open coding—uncovering conceptual categories present in the data (the data's theoretical potential), axial coding—identifying relationships between them, and pursuing a conceptualization of these categories at a higher level of abstraction, which accounts for selective coding (Punch 1998). The latter, as analyzed by Strauss and Corbin (1994), suggests the introduction of two more specific concepts: the core category, as the central phenomenon around which categories are integrated, and the story line, as the descriptive narrative about the central phenomenon, which is analyzed toward an encompassing, abstract conceptualization. The core category was identified as "Jewish identity" (or rather "being Jewish"). It brought about a spectrum of related categories, which all reveal different aspects of Jewish identity, and more specifically of being Jewish in Poland. My "working" categories here were as follows: "Jewish self-definition," "Polish/Jewish," "Polish specificity," "conversion," "authenticity," "primordialism," "what if . . . ," and "mission." I also distinguished a number of sub-categories.

Grounded theory analysis allowed for an emerging and abstract interpretation of what was central in the generated data by categorizing and organizing it according to discernible patterns; thus, it was meant to account for theory development (Punch 1998; Shkedi and Horenczyk 1995; Strauss and Corbin 1994). Throughout the process of categorizing sets of data, there emerged patterns and schemes which allowed for an open-ended recategorization of data in light of shifting conceptual frameworks, social contexts, and a continuing self-reflexivity (Mason 1996).

Inasmuch as my study deals with ways in which people narrate their experience and offer a large volume of personal records in the form of a story (Denzin 1994; Riessman 1993), I paid attention to form and content in trying to reveal how the participants manage to name meanings and experiences (Coffey and Attkinson 1996; Punch 1998; Spradley 1979). However, it is important for me to note that my analysis does not follow any existing formal rules of narrative analysis or discourse analysis. Although my emphasis is on how individuals construct self-narratives, I maintain a position on identity, which appreciates the significance of narrative and discourse in understanding how people organize their relationships with the world. I agree with Mikhail Bakhtin in that "the single adequate form for *verbally expressing* authentic human existence is the *open-ended dialogue*" (Bakhtin 1984, 293).

> Life by its very nature is dialogic. To live means to participate in dialogue; to ask questions, to heed, to respond, to agree and so forth. In this dialogue a person participates wholly and throughout his whole life. (Bakhtin 1984, 293)

Positioning the Researcher

Writing about Jews in Poland has been a challenge, both academically and personally. I cannot possibly estimate how many times I was asked whether there were any Jews living in Poland. The disbelieving question often already followed my disclosure of the topic of this study. Staszek Krajewski neatly observed that foreigners see the Jewish absence in Poland more clearly than they see "us"—the living Polish Jews (Krajewski 2005).

In this study, I write about Jews who, in the practical sense, grew up as non-Jews. As I mentioned earlier, I too only discovered my Jewish background in young adulthood. I was born in 1978, and I fit all other criteria to qualify as a participant in a study of the third post-Holocaust generation of Polish Jews.

I find it important to emphasize the fact that the implications of the socio-cultural and historical circumstance of the researcher cannot be overestimated in any research (Denzin and Lincoln 1994; Haraway 1991). My position has its advantages and its drawbacks. On the one hand, it facilitated the sampling process. I knew most of the participants personally, and I could access others through the ones I knew. It also gave me the benefit of avoiding potential initial distrust, and I have the impression that it contributed to the general genuineness of my particular participants' narratives. However, it is also my impression that "being one of *them*" possibly entailed some basic assumptions on both sides of the equation. I might have failed to successfully avoid rendering certain pieces of information self-evident in my analysis, and I suppose my participants might have assumed that I know the answers to some of my questions, which could mean that they intentionally condensed their answers during the interview. I can only hope that this was not the case. Nevertheless, I must note that my particular relationship with the participants resulted in a very informal, comfortable, and open style of interviews, which I see as a major advantage. Moreover, being an "insider" perhaps stressed even more the fact that performing this type if research was, also for me, necessarily "identity work" (Coffey 1999), where little is self-evident to me.

With regard to fighting my own limitations, I repeatedly confronted my patterns of analysis with my two advisors, who are Jews, but not from Poland, as well as with two other scholars: a non-Jewish Pole and a non-Polish non-Jew. Their feedback was essential to how I structured the discussion of the results of my research.

RESULTS

Narrating Identity

I make sense of my own identity by telling myself a story about my own life. In neither case is the identity like that of a fixed structure or substance. These identities are mobile. (. . .) Until the story is finished, the identity of each character or person remains open to revision (Dauenhauer 2005).

WHAT CAN BE INFERRED from the above statement is that this study can only aspire to offer a meta-story about a group of people, wherein I can only try to make sense of how they try to make sense of their identities. Such a meta-story or in this case perhaps even a meta-meta-story is a rendering of fluctuating and unfinished "identity slots," time-spatial slots of identity, if you like.

Charles Taylor writes that grasping our lives in a narrative is a "basic condition of making sense of ourselves" (Taylor 1989, 47). Narrative is therefore a necessary means of appreciating meanings in an individual's life. It is not "an optional extra," it is a *sine qua non* (Taylor 1989). Or, as Roland Barthes puts it,

> Narrative is present in every age, in every place, in every society; it begins with the very history of mankind and there nowhere is nor has been a people without narrative. All classes, all human groups have their narratives . . . narrative is international, transhistorical, transcultural: It is simply there, like life itself. (Barthes 1977, 79).

Theory of narrative is rooted in the work of Russian formalists, particularly Vladimir Propp (1968) and Boris Tomashevski (1965) (see also Franzosi 1998). Tomashevski proposed a distinction between story and plot, where the story is the basic chronological and logical order of what happened, whereas the plot is the way in which what happened is arranged and presented to the reader (Tomashevski 1965). This distinction remained applicable when adapted by French structuralists (see Barthes 1977; Toolan 1988) who juxtapose *histoire* versus *discours*. They argue that self and narrative are inseparable, and they use Gerald Edelman's (1989) theory of consciousness with its definition of the self as "an unfolding reflective awareness of being-in-the-world, including a sense of one's past and future" (Edelman 1989, 106). Every "telling" provides an opportunity for a fragmented self-understanding for both the teller and the receiver (or the listener) (Ochs and Capps 1996).

Although, as I mentioned earlier, I do not engage in formal narrative analysis, I want to appreciate and emphasize the fact that there are stories, and there are ways to tell them, and I aim to give ear to the ways in which people tell their stories.

Chronology is a feature of the story, not of the plot. This is not to say that a given plot necessarily avoids chronology. The latter surely provides one of the accessible ways to structure a story. In the interviews, I sought to secure as much freedom as possible for the interviewee to deliver his or her story as he or she knows or remembers it. Not at all surprisingly, only a very general structure can be discerned from the way all of the individual narratives unraveled.

All the participants in this research either knew me personally or had learned about where I was coming from through an intermediary. In effect, they had all made assumptions about the purpose of the interview prior to my first question. As a result of this, the general tendency in the way the interviews advanced was for the interviewees to present to me the story of how it happened that they became interviewees in this study about Jewish identity. In most of the cases, this meant delivering an account of how they learned about their Jewish roots. Again, in most cases, such an account was followed by a description of the processes, which led to embracing a form of Jewish identity.

Two different ways to begin the story transpired. The first one focused on the individual's family—their grandparent or grandparents, often ones the interviewee never had the opportunity to meet. This meant telling the pre-war account of events which explains the Jewish presence in the family history and often consequently its rupture or its renunciation, and only then describing the circumstances in which the individual found out about that Jewish past. The other pattern was that of starting with one's own experience of "the discovery," of learning about one's connection to Jewishness, about an existing family link. Curiously, without entering structural analysis, we can distinguish here between two different approaches to chronology: (1) where time is treated as one, objective, historical, and linear, and where an individual person's history is delivered as part of a larger scheme; and (2) where chronology is perceived in an individual life's perspective, where events are presented according to the order in which they were exposed to the individual, where the past is presented as a subjective part of one's present.

In this study, we can observe intriguing patterns in the ways people see themselves vis-à-vis history and vis-à-vis what some call "fate," and, most importantly, we can learn about the particular individual struggles to make sense of one's existence.

In this section, I present the results of the study. They are divided into sets, which include remarks on the experience of the discovery of Jewish ancestry, with the reactions it caused and some examples of the "first steps" toward more communal Jewish involvement, followed by the interviewees' accounts of their Polishness and their Jewishness and statements about a "sense of mission." The two major sets of results which follow are the participants' views on authenticity and self-authentication (these are divided into a number of subcategories) and the participants' references to primordialist discourse (again, I distinguish a number of sub-categories here). I then present examples of the participants' attempts at possible collective self-definitions and some reflections on the question of antisemitism. Finally, I review the interviewees' statements with regard to their plans for the future. Following the results section, I proceed to discussion and conclusions.

The Discovery

ALL THE PARTICIPANTS IN my study had a story to tell—the story of how it happened that they are now representatives of the third post-Holocaust generation of Polish Jews. Although the individual stories certainly differ, there are multiple common patterns, which the interviewees themselves sought to illustrate.

Most of the interviewees "bumped into" their Jewish roots in their teens. All those who mention that they were in fact aware of them earlier in their childhood maintain that they only "internalized" that knowledge sometime in their teens. In other words, even if they knew all along that, for example, their grandfather was Jewish, they did not really know what being Jewish meant in general, and certainly not what it meant to them. As I mentioned earlier, six of my interviewees have stated that they were always aware of their Jewish roots. However, all six of them also report that they were not raised in Jewish homes and only started learning something about being Jewish in their teens. A number of our participants found out about their Jewish ancestry only in their early twenties.

Allow me to discuss some of the different patterns I identified in the "discovery narratives." First, there are those in which the "secret" was revealed by a parent or grandparent, and those in which the participants themselves discovered it. In the latter case, a "Jewish identity quest" often began with suspicions that led to a search for "evidence."

> I was having a discussion with my father and then he says
> to me listen, your mother is Jewish and . . . I thought he
> was only kidding. (Zofia)

In many cases, the timing or the circumstances in which the parent or grandparent made the decision to reveal the Jewish connection in the family seem quite incidental. Although it has been pointed out that in Eastern Europe Jewish grandparents tend to feel most inclined to reveal their "secrets" on their deathbeds, none of my participants mentioned having such an experience, as circumstantial as it may in fact be. In the majority of our cases, if a grandparent revealed part of the "Jewish secret" at a certain point, he or she would never agree to talk about it again. A number of the interviewees' grandparents are alive to this day and still wish to remain silent. For example, when Joanna confronted her grandmother about the suspicions she had about her Jewish background, she heard, "Yes, it's true, but I don't want to talk about it." Aneta, on the other hand, says she heard her grandmother say something which she interpreted to mean that she was Jewish, but when confronted her grandmother repeatedly denied it. As a result of this, Aneta is convinced that she is Jewish but will most likely never be able to prove it.

Franka recalls simply having "figured out" that there was a Jewish connection in her family when distant relatives came to visit from Israel. Odelia says she found out that her father was Jewish, but his parents do not want to talk about being Jewish and do not want to talk about how they survived in hiding, having received help from Polish Catholics during the Holocaust.

> I looked up my last name in the Internet because it's an unusual name, and it turned out to be a Jewish Hungarian name. (Stella)

Stella continued her research on family ancestry, and although she is convinced that she has Jewish roots, she eventually converted under the auspices of the Conservative movement. Some other stories of the "discovery" include some in which complex family histories or unusual surnames, like Stella's, provoked our participants to perform some sort of research, but also those in which family members would accidentally say something they did not necessarily intend to say, or even some in which someone's "unusual looks" raised suspicions. In a few cases, where the revelation came from a grandparent or where particular information about a grandparent was discovered by the interviewee, it meant that the parent(s), too, were suddenly introduced to new knowledge about their ancestry. In Wiktor's case, his father told him relatively late because he himself had no awareness of his Jewish roots until the age of forty years. Wiktor's grandparents survived the war with the help of two Polish families. For many years after the Holocaust, they chose not to mention their Jewish background.

> We were traveling by train together. And I told my dad
> I was gay, and in return he told me he was Jewish . . . It
> was exciting for me! (Wiktor)

None of our participants recall the moment when they found out about their Jewish ancestry as a negative experience. Clearly, all of the interviewees underwent a major transition and yet interestingly, although for some the very moment may have been a somewhat overwhelming experience, they certainly do not view it as a negative one. Confusing at times, certainly, but not negative. In many interviews, the reason for this became obvious, as some participants described "the discovery" as a natural event, which had an almost relieving effect on them. In other words, they had "a hunch," an irrational feeling, that there was "something there" waiting to be discovered. The participants mention being pleased or even excited about it.

> It was hot! I was terribly proud of it, because I always
> felt that Christianity was dumb—not sure why, so I was
> really thrilled! (Sara)

The citations I want to present now are those that describe the psychological effect of a sudden impression of things making sense. These interviewees claim that they sensed something "wrong," "strange," or "different" about them before they knew they had Jewish roots; therefore, discovering those roots brought a sense of relief and of some kind of subjective logical order to their lives. Eryk describes that feeling of relief in the following way:

> You know, I was relieved, I always felt that there was
> something wrong with me . . . this Jewish identity really
> suited me best. (Eryk)

Adam recalls a similar positive reaction to his introduction to Jewishness.

> From the first moment I met other Jews . . . I felt that

it liberated a sedated part of my personality or identity.
(Adam)

Danuta says she always felt "attracted" to learning about Judaism, long before she was told that her father was Jewish. The following three citations describe the feeling of things turning out according to some "metaphysical order":

> I dug it out, but it was meant to happen, by fate really . . .
> (Natalia)

> It happened [but] I knew it was bound to happen . . . I believe in fate, in that I had to [discover it]. (Stella)

> I realize that it sounds really cheap, but I somehow subconsciously sensed it . . . (Magda)

Łukasz mentions the same feeling but also adds an interesting remark regarding choice.

> I didn't choose it just like that, I think it was something that I was supposed to do. Sooner or later it would have happened, so probably it was supposed to be and so I'm glad about it. (Łukasz)

What Łukasz appears to be saying is that no actual choice was involved in his experience because what he did in looking for ways to become actively Jewish after he found out that his father was Jewish was somehow presupposed. In fact, he suggests an ethical compulsion in that he only did what he "was supposed to do." This is precisely, if I may, "as if" his soul had been at Sinai and the "Jewish spark" in him was simply bound to be rekindled, or as if he had been driven by some form of Kantian categorical imperative which required of him to embrace his Jewishness (Kant 1785).

Natalia says she always reacted to antisemitism very strongly. "Maybe it was in my genes," she wonders now, knowing that she does have Jewish ancestry. She continues,

> I don't know what is in those genes, [but] there's something there. I can't explain it. There are more things in heaven and earth than your philosophers will ever know . . . meaning that there is that place where empirical science ends and a different world begins. I don't know . . . I didn't use to believe in that world and I suppose that discovering [Jewish] roots changed that. (Natalia)

Stella, whose grandfather was Jewish, mentions a slightly different reason for not being surprised about her discovery:

> Even at the time I wasn't Jewish, most of my close friends were Jews. (Stella)

Joanna suggests that what she came to discover accounted for her being "different" all along.

> It's positive, because if something was sitting inside of you . . . even if you didn't know that you were a little different . . . (Joanna)

Notice that "difference" is perceived as something positive. Sara also implies that her Jewish roots are "responsible" for how she always felt, and once again "being different" is described as a positive feature. Jewishness is perceived to be a valuable mark of distinction.

> I always felt different, I always felt alienated. (Sara)

Similarly, Natalia believes her Jewish identity "had to come out." She mentions a particularly interesting conflict between reason and emotions. What Natalia describes is feeling something which her own reasoning nevertheless questions.

> Somewhere inside me something was going on, so it had to come out. When I look back at this whole journey, I can say that it couldn't have been otherwise, that that's what it's all about. On the other hand though, I'm in psychology—a science, so on one side I have this mysti-

cism and on the other that empiricism, and they don't go together, but somehow they coexists within me, inside. (Natalia)

Some participants also mention that they finally understood why they looked the way they looked. These were normally rather humorous statements: a few interviewees mentioned their noses and dark hair, and some female participants even mentioned their hips. As peculiar as it may be, the rhetoric of looking or not looking Jewish is widely present in the narratives of the participants. It may be important to mention that "Jewish looks" are in fact considered a rare and generally much coveted "commodity" among the representatives of the third generation.

In her article "'Funny, You Don't Look Jewish': Visual Stereotypes and the Making of Modern Jewish Identity," Susan Glenn points to the paradoxes of the discourse of "looking Jewish" and notices how such "primordial concepts" are used not only by hostile "others" but by Jews themselves (Glenn 2010).

The process of discovering Jewish roots is described as a positive experience by all of our participants. The different accounts included expressions such as "very positive," "I felt terribly proud," "I was glad," "fascinating," "exciting," or "awesome." It is necessary to note at this point that our sample comprises people who pursued a form of Jewish identity following "the discovery." It does not include people who may have found out about their Jewish roots and ignored it. It is fair to assume that there are young adult Poles out there whose reaction to their Jewish roots is anywhere between neutral and negative and who accordingly do not pursue a Jewish identity. They remain beyond the scope of this study. They may in fact be unidentifiable for any study, because they choose to obscure their Jewish connection. Little can be said of them with any scientific validity, but perhaps it is of value to mention that in the third generation many of us have had the opportunity to come across one or two people who know they have Jewish ancestry but do not choose to do anything about this knowledge. The general impression though is that there are statistically few of them in the same age group and that we are more likely to meet people who feel inspired by our stories to the extent that they too desire to undertake some steps toward discovering their own potential Jewish roots. And in a place like Poland, such steps often go a long way.

Aside from the generally positive responses to the discovery of Jewish roots, what seems to transpire in the narratives is a common uncanny feeling of having "something inside," that indescribable intrinsic attribute, a mark of difference. Once again, the primordial experience at Sinai comes to mind. In the perception of our participants, it was only a matter of time before they would discover their Jewish roots because they always felt that "there was something there," waiting to be discovered.

The history of obscuring Jewish family background in Poland, of turning it into a deep secret, goes back more than two generations. Young Jews in Poland often learn about how their great-grandparents made conscious efforts to "pass for Poles" as early as in the last decades of the nineteenth century. In some cases, including my own, "the secret" remained "safe" within the family throughout most of the twentieth century, and it seemed unimaginable that someone would come along and "dig it out." Between World War II and the early 1990s, there was no right time for people to deliberately "come out" as Jews in Poland. For the generation of our parents and grandparents, to identify as a Jew was nothing but a stigma. Of course, there are still Jews in Poland today who associate their Jewishness with a stigma. But for most young people who began their identity quest in the 1990s or later, Jewishness is a primarily positive experience. Fear has been ingrained in the Polish lands for so long that it may take many more decades before people definitively stop dreading a Jewish identification. The third generation is one that begins this process in many ways for everyone else—for older generations of Jews, but perhaps also for Poles who themselves still have some difficulty uttering the word "Jew." I'll come back to this issue later.

The discovery of Jewish roots is just a starting point for the representatives of the third post-Holocaust generation of Jews in Poland. What happens next is a long process of having to actively socialize themselves into Jewishness and "figure themselves out" as Jews. In other words, they embark on a journey from a Jewish identification to a Jewish identity. First, they discover *that* they are Jewish and then they try to discover themselves as Jews—they discover *how* they will be Jewish.

There are many common themes in the individual accounts of "what happened next" or, in other words, of the first steps in the pursuit of Jewishness.

> I found the [Jewish] community and I suddenly saw that
> there are Polish Jews out there. (Teresa)

Wiktor recalls that the "urge to do something" about his Jewishness appeared as soon as he met another person in Krakow who also had a Jewish father. Together they started organizing activities for people with Jewish roots. Szymon recalls that the first step he took was studying Jewish philosophy (he was at the time majoring in the history of philosophy). Simultaneously, Szymon began attending synagogue, where he met other people like himself and learned more about Judaism. Danuta's first steps also involved looking for people who shared her experience.

> After I found out, I wanted to take some more active
> moves, not just to read books, but to meet live Jews in
> Poland, to see how it all looks in Poland . . . how it is in
> Israel, how it is in the Jewish world in general. (Danuta)

Similarly, Ewelina describes how she found other Jews.

> It turned out that there are plenty of people . . . who are
> just like me . . . at first glance—nothing in common, but
> you know, once we started telling each other the differ-
> ent stories of how we got there . . . (Ewelina)

Hana describes a very similar impression from becoming acquainted with other young Polish Jews.

> There was this group of people who have similar experi-
> ences, and completely different ones, but nonetheless
> . . . we have something in common, we are not alone in
> the world, we share something, each one of us could find
> someone within that group who had an identical story,
> that we are not alone. (Hana)

Teresa mentions that when she first met other Jews in Poland she felt that she met people who were just as lost as she was. Aleksandra talks about "common experiences," "common histories," and about "feeling at home." To sum up, a common pattern in the participants' experience emerged—namely, the initial stages of Jewish involvement took shape through interaction with other people who shared their "condition."

> Our parents told us about the family secret, but they didn't give us any direction . . . they left us all alone with this, thinking that it's enough to just tell, but they didn't show us any way to deal with it . . . (Alan)

> I grew up convinced that I was the only Jew in Wroclaw. (Alex)

Alex explains that it was not until he met a girl who also had Jewish roots that he actually realized that there is a possibility of a Jewish communal belonging for him. Together with his brother, he embarked on a journey which, within a few years, brought them to a point where they made a conscious decision to reclaim their grandfather's last name. They both ended up changing their Polish-sounding name—one that their grandfather had adopted for himself—to the original Jewish-sounding name he had relinquished in order to pass for a Pole. Historically speaking, we must appreciate that this is a totally unprecedented phenomenon. Never before in Polish history—or perhaps in European history—have Jews deliberately taken on more Jewish-sounding names. It is in that sense a profoundly de-assimilationist act. It is one of the most explicit forms of Jewish "coming out" in the modern world.

> I think an important characteristic of Polish Jewish identity is the fact that we socialize through relationships with our peers, that we are a generation which didn't have family Pesach Seders and for most of us one of the basic experiences in the transmission of Jewish identity was the first Passover Seder organized by some of our more experienced peers. (Alex)

Alex goes on to say that it took him four years to achieve enough "Jewish literacy" to run a Passover Seder, and when he eventually did, it made him "very proud."

BEING POLISH

WITH THE DISCOVERY OF Jewish roots and the subsequent pursuit of Jewish identity, our participants were faced with the need to reconcile two identities: Polish and Jewish. According to the narratives, embracing Jewishness does not change the fact that Polishness remains a significant element of the participants' identities. The interviews showed that there is a general sense of attachment to Poland shared by the participants. Significant differences can be distinguished as to what type of attachment is at stake. When asked about feeling Polish, the interviewees mention the evident facts of being born in Poland, raised in Poland, and being exposed to Polish as the primary language.

> I am emotionally attached to this country because this is where I was born and raised, because I speak Polish. (Elza)

This is indicative of a self-evident attachment provided by the givens of being born in a specific environment and into a concrete language as well as having been nurtured in that place and in that language. As for other aspects of culture, none of the participants pointed to Catholicism as having an influence on their identity, though in fact most of them had direct contact with the Polish Catholic tradition. The elements of Polish culture that were mentioned as the significant factors for the individual identities were literature and (in a number of cases) the socio-cultural implications of the Polish experience of the communist regime and the struggle against it. A few other idiosyncratic characteristics of being Polish also appeared in the narratives. One example is the image of Poles as people who do not cease to complain.

> I like to complain. I like the fact that Poles complain— they are world champions in complaining, it is our national sport. I like this kind of pessimism mixed with a touch of irony and sarcasm. (Franka)

Sarcasm, we must say, is ever-present in the way young people in Poland talk to each other—this of course being more of a personal observation than a scientific one. I might add that there exists a popular perception of Israelis as people who complain a lot. There also exists a plethora of stereotypes of Polish Jewish women in Israel who are believed to be pessimistic, worrying, and overly critical of everything and everyone. We can see more of such self-irony in the following citation.

> Am I a Polish Jew? Sure, because I am also this complaining Jew, who doesn't particularly like his congregation, who has problems with everyone around him, who would maybe be willing to change, if only you gave me a chance . . . and that constant complaining! (Ewelina)

Only one of my interviewees has two Jewish parents each of whom has two Jewish parents. Although the family members were aware of their Jewishness, they did nothing about it, and my interviewee only realized that she was in fact a Jew herself in her late teens. Symptomatic as it may be for most of our participants to have only "fragmentary" Jewish ancestry, one has to emphasize the distinct implications of having Polish, non-Jewish family members. Trivial as it may sound, having Polish family is an important factor conditioning the individuals' relationships to Polishness.

> I definitely identify as a Jew. But I don't negate the past and everything that happened over the years, I mean being raised in Poland, in a Polish family. (Natalia)

> I think it's important that I identify as a Polish Jew and that I didn't reject the fact that I'm Polish. (Joanna)

The interviewees talk about an emotional attachment to aspects of Polish history and emphasize the importance of shared experiences with other Polish people, mainly family and friends. What they do not seem to express is a sense of nationhood, of belonging to the Polish nation as a whole.

There is definitely a connection with the country, with the language, with the people who live here, [but] as far as national identity goes or whatever you might call it it's still some sort of mystery for me. (Szymon)

[I feel Polish] to a great extent, I mean I do feel that despite this whole baggage of disdain and of being pissed off at this country, I nevertheless feel that it is my country, that this is where I grew up. (Wiktor)

Eryk mentions the importance of Poland as a place:

I feel an identification with the place, but not with nationality. (Eryk)

Here, once again, we can see that whether it is place, language, family, friends, history, or literature, our participants nevertheless do not express a strong identification with the Polish nation as a whole.

What transpires here is that we tend to have the impression that it is other people who have cultures, while ours seems to be invisible to us. This was observed by Vincent J. Cheng (2004), who also wonders whether what he calls "heritage industry" or "roots mania" are ways to overcome the feeling of inauthenticity or of dullness of our own culture and identity. It remains debatable here whether it is anxiety over culture and identity that brings about root searching or whether it is the discovery of roots that brings about identity transition. In any regard, one of the most striking findings here is that, for most of our participants, Polishness seems to have become "an issue" only following the discovery and exploration of Jewishness. Another way to put it would be to say that it was after they started "becoming Jewish" that they actually "noticed" their "being Polish" and started wondering about the meaning of Polishness to them. Alongside their construction of Jewish identity, a discussion of Polish identity was provoked. By the same token, all of our interviewees' narratives indicate an existing dialectic of Polishness and Jewishness as the two are constantly measured up against one another.

There is no such thing as simply Jewish identity. I mean,

it's terribly limiting. Identity is influenced by millions of things, identity is influenced by how we dress, who we spend time with, by education, etc. And so it is also influenced by Jewish ancestry. I mean, it can be. My identity is certainly influenced by Jewish ancestry, but it is also influenced by the fact that I was born in Poland. . . . Identity is a blend of many things [and] there is no reason that I shouldn't be such a Polish Jewish blend. (Robert)

Most of our participants talked about the dialectic of Polishness and Jewishness, and although many view it as a challenge, it is nevertheless one that they willingly undertake. Generally, then, the interviewees identify with both Polishness and Jewishness. They talk about Polishness and Jewishness as two entirely different types of identification. It is still the case, however, that it is Jewishness that is the identification more likely to be questioned by others as well as by the participants themselves.

I don't have to wonder which side is better and which one I should pursue. I am Polish and Jewish in a parallel way and that is how it's going to be. (Magda)

As far as Polishness being confronted by Jewishness, none of the interviewees told me that they felt less Polish as soon as they realized they had Jewish ancestry. Perhaps a better way to put it would be to say that the Jewish element altered Polishness, but did not diminish it.

[After I discovered I was Jewish] I didn't feel less Polish in the least. I felt that I now had a kind of addition to being Polish. (Zofia)

[Being Jewish and being Polish] . . . are not mutually exclusive things. (Robert)

I am a Pole and a Jew. For me, these two identities don't bother one another. (Greg)

I wouldn't want a different background. I'm not ashamed of who I am. On the contrary, I am happy about who I am, and part of who I am is in my Jewish and in my Polish ancestry. (Max)

In the narratives, Polishness and Jewishness are described as two identities which need not be mutually exclusive. The following are the participants' accounts of their individual understandings of being Jewish.

BEING JEWISH

THE WORD "IDENTITY" IS not as commonly used in Polish as it is in English. Moreover, in Polish, it has the reputation of a slightly pompous academic term and even those of my interviewees who are students in the humanities used it scarcely and somewhat reluctantly. Nevertheless, identity as an idea was present in every interview. I find it important to mention that I made conscious efforts not to resort to the "I" word in my questions, although I tried to remain alert to it coming up in the answers.

I identified two general lay approaches to the concept of identity. The two approaches are parallel to the theoretical distinction offered earlier. Namely, one approach is of an essentialist nature, along the lines of positivist definitions of identity as given, inherited, and primordial. The other approach endorses the fluid, multi-dimensional, internally diverse and constructed nature of identity or of Jewish identity. Our participants spoke more of Jewish identity than they did of identity in general, which is understandable in our context. An example of the essentialist approach is represented in the following statement by Sara, who was raised as a Catholic, then found out that her father was Jewish and underwent conversion to Judaism, becoming an observant Orthodox Jewish woman:

> I cannot imagine that I could change my life like this for something that doesn't concern me family-wise . . . for something, which isn't connected with some responsibility of mine . . . I cannot imagine that I would show up from nowhere and say: "I want to be Jewish," not because it's something bad, but it's a different type of thinking about identity. (Sara)

This seems to suggest that while Sara undoubtedly underwent a process of transition, she nevertheless refuses to see it in terms of choice.

It becomes clearer yet in the interview that the decision to convert stemmed from a sense of responsibility to repay a debt to her Jewish grandparents and to continue their Judaism. Sara's father did not choose to lead a religious or even traditional Jewish life. Paradoxically, Sara sees her entire transition from a Polish-Catholic life to a Jewish-Orthodox one in terms of something she "had to do," not in terms of a choice she made. For her, the identity she embraced is, despite all, an imperative one. She feels that she had no other choice but to embrace it. At the same time, she stresses the fact that she would never consider converting to Judaism if she had no Jewish roots. The decision to be religious is seen as a strong commitment, as being Jewish "all the way." Similar approaches will be discussed later in the context of the relationship between primordialism and authenticity. Let us, however, look at some examples of the practically opposite view of identity transition.

> It was completely and exclusively a decision, a choice to do something about it [about Jewish roots], there was no pressure at all, and I can imagine my life had I not made that choice . . . , but I wanted this, and that's the decision I made. (Aleksandra)

We can see here that while Sara's approach is of a determinist nature, Aleksandra makes every effort to rationalize her experience as she stresses her personal "executive" autonomy. Like Sara, Aleksandra has a Jewish father. Another example is that of Eryk.

> I have this freedom of choice now, who I want to be . . . I feel good about it. If it had been imposed on me in childhood, then I don't know [if I would want to be Jewish] . . . (Eryk)

In this case, Eryk, whose father is Jewish, suggests that the reason he identifies as a Jew today is precisely because it came to him as an option he could reject or embrace. Here, the fact of Jewish identity not being a given becomes a value in itself. Elza mentions another aspect in what could be labeled as an existentialist approach to Jewish identity, where self-identification is the main factor.

> If someone feels Jewish that's already great. It doesn't matter if it's after the mother or the father. (Elza)

The fact that it is a struggle to pursue a Jewish identity which one was not raised with, is a self-evident statement. To try to capture this struggle in words is most difficult, for both the participants and the researcher. Our sample consists of people who did undertake the pursuit of some form of Jewish identity. In the Polish context, this also meant that ready models of Jewish identity were scarce and much less accessible than in "normal" Jewish communities.

> [I was Polish] but I knew nothing about Jewishness, so as a way of filling that void in my life I decided that I would be Jewish, because I didn't know it. I want to learn, I find it important that it is somehow my heritage, but it's more emotional than it is rational, so it's difficult to say how one can make such a decision . . . I just felt that it was something I should do. (Franka)

Again, in this case we can see the prevalent approach to being Jewish, which perceives it in emotional terms as an imperative rather than a rational choice. In the following two statements, special emphasis is put on the social aspect of Jewish identity.

> There are so many dimensions of this [Jewish] identity, and damn it, I don't know yet where I'll end up. It is a problem how to define a Jew, I still haven't figured out how to define a Jew, what it is, who it really is, is it a nationality, is it a religion . . . well it's not religion and it's not necessarily nationality. . . . I think it's a social belonging and that's how I see it, as my place in some kind of community, identifying oneself with a group . . . and I see Jews as my group. . . . Being Jewish is different for every person. (Natalia)

> Until recently, I had no idea what this concept of identity was about. (. . .) I embraced an identity that isn't

there. My personal identity does not depend on history, and not on Israel, but rather on what is here—at Twarda [name of the street where the Jewish Community in Warsaw is located], in Wroclaw, in Krakow, it's where I am and where I meet people. (Marek)

Another important observation, which follows from the previous citations, is that the participants view their Jewish identities as contextualized—as situated in the specific Polish context.

The following is a citation from Teresa, who seems to lean toward a more conservative approach to Jewish identity.

I believe that I must protect my tradition, and that my tradition is important to me, that I can't be ashamed of it, that I can't hide it. I am part of this nation and that it [Judaism] is my religion. (Teresa)

Teresa does not define herself as religious. In fact, she repeatedly mentioned the fact that she is not a religious person. Nevertheless, not only does she stress the religious component but also somehow identifies with it. Her statement can be contrasted with that of Bożena's, who leads a relatively observant Jewish life.

Being Jewish doesn't depend on being religious or not. (Bożena)

This reads as though, regardless of her personal preferences, Bożena does not identify being Jewish with religion.

As indicated earlier, among our fifty participants, ten are religiously observant or are considering living a more observant Jewish life. Only two of these were born to Jewish mothers, whereas the remaining eight either converted to Judaism or intend to do so in the near future. I have identified a small number of participants who have experienced and continue to experience "religious episodes," that is, they had periods in their life when they would qualify as observant Jews, and it remains unclear whether they will end up being observant or not in the future. Among them are persons who do not have a Jewish mother and may consider formal conversion. The remaining participants identify as nonreligious, although some of them perform certain Jewish rituals (such as lighting candles on Shabbat), and/or observe a degree of kashrut—Jewish dietary laws. For example, some choose to refrain from eating pork.

The following are some examples of the prevalent non-religious attitude:

> I guess it's not the right lifestyle for me, being religious . . . (Ewelina)

> Why should I be religious if I don't feel it, I don't feel it at all. (Joanna)

Similarly, Eryk mentions that his identification with Jewishness is not a religious one, but an "ethnic" one. Generally, all participants, including the religious ones, stressed the ethnic or cultural components of Jewishness as central to their understanding of being Jewish. However, Judaism as a tradition, as a system of values, and perhaps less so as a system of rules to follow, was an important reference in the identity narratives.

Among the remarks about identity or Jewish identity made by the participants are several that do and several that do not try to define it.

> My Jewishness is in spending time with people, in identifying with my roots and in . . . not in boasting about it, but in talking about it openly. (Patrycja)

> To be Jewish in Poland is to create Jewish life—from scratch, a completely different one and on a smaller scale, but that doesn't mean that it is a lesser one. (Alex)

> It is something new in my life and it gives me certain possibilities, and it is something I can further explore. And it is something, which gives me "me" and helps me to learn more about me. (Zofia)

For me, to be a Jew is not to speak Hebrew or pray in synagogue. For me, to be a Jew is to be a descendant of one of five million people who lived between Moscow and Berlin a hundred years ago. Those are my Jews. That is my identity. (Max)

SENSE OF MISSION

DURING MY INQUIRY, IT became clear that in the narratives of the participants, the idea of being Jewish in Poland is commonly associated with "a sense of mission." It involved a closer analysis to uncover the different types of "mission" that the participants' narratives exposed. To be clear, some interviewees strongly reject the notion of mission in their discourse—they simply do not like the word. However, as is revealed in the narratives, regardless of the wording, they generally refer to what I labeled as a "sense of mission"—for lack of a better term.

The most visible manifestations of a sense of mission come from an appreciation of the particular historical gravity of the Polish Jewish experience. In other words, the interviewees make concrete statements about the Shoah as one of the main factors determining the specificity of the Jewish existence in Poland after World War II. They repeatedly mention the destruction of Polish Jewry as having a direct impact on their families' histories. They also emphasize what a great and flourishing community the Polish Jewish community once was. Significantly, the dominant impression we can acquire from the interviews is that the Holocaust is acknowledged as a fundamental factor which shaped the trajectories of post-war Jewish experience in Poland. However, the participants in this study do not necessarily perceive it as a defining component of their individual identities.

The following quotations illustrate the idea of "mission," described as a sense of responsibility to continue Jewish existence in Poland. Indications of this kind of sense of mission were present in all of the conducted interviews. Although at some times expressed less lucidly than at others, the renderings of this sense of mission are one of the most interesting findings of my research.

> I feel that I am a descendant of those times. I feel that I owe something to those people who died, I constantly feel that I must live for them, that it is for them that I

must restore the Jewish world . . . I feel that it is my duty to exist and to do everything I can for that culture and that people to live on. (Teresa)

Needless to say, the sense of mission is frequently associated with the Holocaust, which in itself is a significant element in the participants' narratives.

Many Jews perished and so when someone finds out that they're Jewish, there is this switch, some kind of diodes in his brain . . . that because so many Jews perished, it has to be repaired. (Patrycja)

It's this against-all-odds kind of thing, you wanted to destroy us but it didn't work. (. . .) I think it's very important for Jewish life in Poland to continue. (Danuta)

I want to continue that, which got lost somewhere . . . which was interrupted. And I know that I am doing a good thing, for myself, and in their memory. (Hana)

Beyond the idea of "filling in" for those who are no longer, of paying homage to the dead, there is the challenge of being Jewish specifically in Poland. Again, it is connected to the destruction of Polish Jewry, but —first and foremost—it involves confronting the prevailing worldwide opinion that there is no Jewish life in Poland, that there will not be one, and that there *should* not be one.

I live here. I want to build Jewishness in Poland, it is my country and it is my mission. (Odelia)

I feel responsible for Jewish continuity in Poland. (Bożena)

Among all of the participants, there is then the conviction that there should be a Jewish community in Poland, and more importantly, they acknowledge that it is largely up to them whether there will be one.

The fact that I live here now . . . that there was a strong

and important Jewish culture here once, and that it was all severed. That is the most vivid image for me. (Wiktor)

It has always been here, and I think that because everything was destroyed, [Jewish] culture, Jewish life in Poland, I would like to be able to do something in order for it to nevertheless exist. (Łukasz)

I want our processes of defining our identity to be visible—to be visible for us, for Americans—for Jews, and for Poles. (Bożena)

Another aspect of the decision to pursue Jewishness in Poland and of being visible is the idea of challenging people's stereotypes and lack of understanding.

The Jewish element in Poland can shake that homogenous perspective a little and bring in a positive ferment and help everyone—Jews all over the world—to understand that Jewish life is possible everywhere and that Poland is not just a land of Jewish cemeteries, and Poles— to understand that there can be many shades of being Polish. (Alex)

Although it remains a struggle to confront other Jews' understanding of being Jewish in Poland, the idea is also to be visible to non-Jewish Poles, which suggests confronting potential antisemitism and perhaps even more so, promoting an awareness of Jewish existence in Poland. It means also to fill in the image of what it means to be a Jew in contemporary Poland and to challenge the existing stereotypes and imagined ideals. This shows that we can in fact talk about a sense of "historical mission," a mission to appropriate a role in history, to pay tribute to the past by creating a present and a future.

In terms of Jewishness in Poland, I believe that we have something that we can build on, because until now everyone kept it a secret. But now there is a group of people and it can grow from it . . . (Odelia)

> The Holocaust happened, but Jews survived and they
> still exist. It's not a matter of restoring what once was,
> but of having Jewish things now, we need that, which is
> right now. (Adam)

Adam's statement seems to call for a move beyond mere nostalgia. He encourages working toward an "authentically Jewish" present. The idea here is that there were always Jews in Poland and that through discovering their Jewish roots the participants were given the opportunity, but even more so the responsibility. to restore Jewish presence in Poland. They "owe it to history" as Max puts it. They owe it to history to be, to exist in Poland as Jews. Because it is Poland, because there nobody will do it for them, because however ambiguous their Jewishness may be in the eyes of the outside world, they nevertheless are the very members of the new generation of Polish Jews.

> I am Jewish because I have Jewish roots, and I decided to
> follow them and save Polish Jews from destruction, that
> is at least to save myself and to educate others. (Bożena)

The idea of saving oneself is accompanied here by the idea of saving other people with Jewish roots "from a non-Jewish life." Adam says he perceives every person of Jewish origin as a "potential Jew." He goes on to say,

> This is why I see it as my personal duty, in Poland, to do
> everything I can to save such a person. (Adam)

As far as the idea of continuity goes, the references were made to the Jewish past, Jewish tradition, Jewish culture, Jewish heritage, or Jewish life. Significantly fewer references were made to concrete family members or specific family history. This is because most of the interviewees know little or nothing about their Jewish ancestors. Be that as it may, I would like to mention some of the more emotional family references.

> To somehow continue my grandparents, to be able to say
> that they didn't die completely, that someone remem-

bers them . . . I am their continuation . . . After all that's happened I can't just sit around and wait . . . I have to fight. (Sara)

Here, we can see a more immediate idea of continuity, of being part of the actual genealogical chain.

The fact that I'm sitting here today is a result of the fact that my grandparents survived the Holocaust, literally, even if nobody in my family ever said a word about it . . . (Marek)

It is a concrete family, a concrete tradition, and there is some kind of responsibility for it, that one cannot forget it, ignore it or leave it. (Sara)

The following two citations show that some interviewees talk about their pursuit of Jewishness, as if it were "despite" their family history. In other words, they mention becoming involved in Jewish life, which their grandparents had rejected.

Fine, so it was my grandparents' or my grandmothers' choice that she gave up Jewishness completely, but it's not the way it has to be with me . . . I have the right and the possibility to build something different, something new. (Aleksandra)

I feel as if I am discovering something, not even for my father, but for my grandmother, you could say, even for my great-grandmother. I am this late wave of that, which apparently most people in my family wanted to put an end to. (Wiktor)

The interviews also indicated that there is a sense of responsibility to pursue knowledge of Jewishness and Judaism, that it is a responsibility of a Jewish person to be able to talk about being Jewish with other people, including non-Jews.

If you're a Jew, then obviously you can't just be indifferent to it, so many people died in the war, most of the
Jewish people were murdered, and so you feel different,
you want to deepen the fact that you are different than
everyone else, that you are original in that way, that you
have [Jewish] roots, and when someone asks you a question: "So tell me something about it, tell me something
about this community, tell me something about this religion," you won't say "Umm, actually . . . I know nothing
. . ." (Patrycja)

Here, the idea to learn is the idea of "owning" one's Jewishness
through an actual understanding of what Judaism and Jewish tradition
stand for. The mission then is to be educators, to be the ones who know
best because they "own" it through their "roots." Notably, the citation
also evokes the compelling element in embracing Jewish identity, which
is rendered here as something one "can't remain indifferent to." Another
"sense of mission" is described as a responsibility to preserve and transmit the memory of the Holocaust.

To be a Jew, to be a Jew from here, yes, from Warsaw,
from this city where you walk on corpses, where you walk
on human skulls, yes . . . This is no ordinary city, this is
the New Jerusalem . . . It's not an ordinary city; it's a
very important city, and a very important country . . .
It is that feeling that this is your legacy, that you cannot
forget, that it is important and that nobody will remember it for you. I have a part in the legacy of the Holocaust
and my part in it is to try to understand. I ought to, I
feel that I should, I feel this responsibility, this duty .
. . to remember, to think about it, to understand, and
to somehow transmit that memory. It is some kind of
absurd reaffirmation of the covenant. (Max)

Max goes on to make a seemingly coarse statement, which in my
view is a rather reflective and a profoundly existential one.

Young Jews in Poland drink beer and nobody else can do

it for them. And in that sense they can feel important, very important. (Max)

What Max appears to be saying is that the mission the members of the third generation of Jews have in Poland is essentially to exist. As in the previous citation from him, it evokes the Shakespearian "to be or not to be," and the mission of young Polish Jews is "to be." In that sense, he points out that the most important thing here is the sole idea that there can be another generation of free (beer-drinking) Jews in Poland and that whether they do anything beyond drinking beer together is secondary to the very fact that they simply are, that they exist against everyone's boldest expectations.

AUTHENTICITY

Certificate of Authenticity

THE IDEA OF AUTHENTICITY became a central one in contemporary discussions on Jewish identity. As we have shown in the introductory chapter, the notion of authenticity appears not only in various interpretations and different academic disciplines and different theories but also in different individual lay renderings. On the one hand then, our interest in authenticity stems from an appreciation of it being a category which is more and more commonly used in debates on identity and Jewish identity. On the other hand, though, the notion of authenticity turned out to be very poignant in the personal narratives of the participants in this study. Authenticity appeared in a number of different contexts, and different individual understandings of it have been presented.

The notion of authenticity appears on a daily basis in the often prosaic situations in which we are forced to prove or confirm that we are who we claim we are—we provide login names and passwords on Internet sites and identification numbers or cards in banks, offices, or libraries. These situations are numerous, and we normally do not reflect on them. In the stories of the participants in our research, we detected a somewhat less prosaic circumstance of having to "authenticate one's Jewishness." Here, we are dealing with a need to provide tangible proof of the Jewish roots one claims he or she has. In other words, presenting appropriate documents is the guarantor of one's identity's authenticity. The participants commonly expressed discontent regarding this issue. For example, Robert says, "It really pisses me off me that I have to prove my ancestry."

It is a practical problem for many representatives of the third post-Holocaust generation of Jews in Poland that whatever Jewish roots they have (parent, grandparent, or further), they are generally unable to locate any tangible evidence of them. They cannot "authenticate" their Jewish roots with appropriate written documents. Needless to say, many of the civil documents in Poland, whether Jewish or Polish, were destroyed during World War II. Some documents were destroyed by Jews themselves out of fear of being persecuted. Moreover, many of the participants' grandparents were not actually born within the borders of today's Poland but often in areas that are now the Ukraine, Hungary, Romania, Belarus, Germany, or Lithuania. Looking for documents which may or may not have survived the war in those countries is an arduous endeavor with little promise of success. However, since 1994 the Jewish Historical Institute in Warsaw runs a genealogy center which dedicates much of its work to "Jewish roots search." Other genealogical projects and workshops have taken place in other Polish cities in the recent years. For example, the Krakow JCC organized Jewish genealogy workshops as part of the Jewish Culture Festival in 2012.

Those who indeed manage to uncover some "papers," which prove their family background, are considered the lucky ones. Interestingly, a number of the "lucky ones" have told me that while they have "the papers for," say, their father, they have reason to believe that their mother was also born to a Jewish mother, although they were not lucky enough to have found "hard evidence" of that. This quandary with documents can often create real difficulties for Polish Jews. One of them is potential immigration to Israel. The Israeli Law of Return grants citizenship to all those who have at least one Jewish grandparent (the prospective citizen must also not be a member of a religion other than Judaism), but it requires unequivocal written proof of it. This often presents a setback for people from Poland. It is important to emphasize that the most common strategy Jews employed to survive the Holocaust in Poland was to try to pass as Christian Poles. In many cases, this involved formally converting to Christianity, and only some people managed to arrange Gentile papers without actually joining the Church through baptism. Hence, many of the interviewees' parents and grandparents have in fact been baptized but, more importantly, so have as many as forty of our fifty participants. Ironically, although nobody asked them whether they wanted to be baptized or not, they are—if only in the light of Israeli immigration law—"members of a different religion." Different interpretations of this law come to play in different countries' Jewish Agency offices. There are records, however, of cases where individuals coming from Poland have been refused Israeli citizenship because of their Jewish ancestors' baptisms. In consequence, those who choose to emigrate to Israel by the Law of Return, if asked whether they (or their Jewish parent or grandparent) were baptized, feel compelled to—for lack of a better word—lie. Baptism was one of the most common survival strategies in Nazi-occupied Poland. The absurd situation is that according to Israel's immigration laws, those who did manage to survive the Holocaust in this way are theoretically not eligible for an *aliyah* ("ascent" in Hebrew, meaning also immigration to Israel).

Perhaps the following example best describes the bitter irony and the frustration "verifying" one's Jewishness may involve.

> I was offered to go on Birthright [sponsored heritage trips to Israel for youth of Jewish descent between 18 and 26] . . . But that involved proving my Jewish roots. So I told them I could show them a picture of my grandfather's dick . . . and if that doesn't satisfy them . . . ! Having to look for some kind of documents is just humiliating for me. (Max)

Another problem for those who cannot satisfactorily prove their roots is a form of internal social disadvantage. In other words, there is a level of initial distrust and condescension toward such members of the community. It is part of the daily discourse among our participants not only to ask who is Jewish or "how Jewish" they are but also to question one's own Jewishness.

The stories of the participants in my study are situated in a sociocultural milieu which has been receiving much attention, relatively speaking, in academic circles, as well as in the media. An aura of inauthenticity has accompanied the processes associated with the so-called "Renaissance of Jewish Culture in Europe" during the past two decades. Non-Jews have become involved in the production of Jewish artifacts, European countries with a "difficult" Jewish past have become "suspiciously" interested in promoting Jewish culture, and "Jewish things" have become "cool" or "trendy." My research shows, however, that while these phenomena are part of the context in which our participants construct their identities, they are not phenomena in terms of which we should explain their identities. In a 1997 *New York Times Magazine* article entitled "Poland's New Jewish Question," Ian Buruma (1997) describes Judaism in Poland as a "new form of chic." Cheng (2004) refers to the notion of "Jewish chic" as well. Jewishness, he claims, represents a "real," concrete identity—an essence, which is imagined to have survived in the global world of "white-bread inauthenticities" (Cheng 2004, 105). He writes about Poland and its particular manifestation of "Jewish chic" as a form of cultural nostalgia which only reinforces essentialist stereotypes of cultural otherness. I have mentioned Ruth Ellen Gruber's less pessimistic assertion that we are in fact dealing with the creation of "new authenticities" or "real imagined spaces," which are different from the "realities" they try to evoke, but are nevertheless in themselves real (Gruber 2009). What I would like to argue is that the construction of Jewish identities of the third post-Shoah generation of Jews in Poland is closely linked to and influenced by the reality of the Polish Jewish "revival" or—as some would call it—"chic." What the stories of my interviewees reveal is a whole other dimension of the question of authenticity. Alongside the widespread concerns about the authenticity of the so-called renaissance of Jewish culture in Poland came the concerns about the authenticity of the younger generation's Jewish identity. And it is in response to those concerns that some of the most poignant statements surfaced in my interviews, accounting for much of the characteristics of Jewish identity construction in contemporary Poland which were yielded by my analysis.

Let me begin with a simple and perhaps even self-evident distinction: my study has shown that people tend to have separate understandings of their own authenticity and of the authenticity of others.

Sense of Authenticity vis-à-vis Oneself

The aura of inauthenticity, which I mentioned before, has become an important factor also in how the participants in this study perceive their own identities. Individual sense of authenticity or lack of thereof can be influenced by existing opinions. Different forms of self-questioning have surfaced in the interviews. My impression is that because of the very specific situation of young Polish Jews (being a relatively new community, and—as I mentioned earlier—being particularly exposed to scrutiny by other Jewish groups, but also non-Jews), most of the examples of self-questioning I am about to present are more or less conscious responses to outside attempts to question the processes of Jewish identity construction in contemporary Poland. In other words, individual concerns about one's own authenticity often appear to be internalized forms of other people's concerns, which the participants were exposed to through conversation or reading.

> I had long wondered what this being Jewish meant, what attracted me in it. Is it some kind of romanticism with regard to the war and to loss of family, or with regard to the fact that from something negative Jews had turned into something positive, into some kind of fashion . . . I could not answer all this for myself. (Sara)

We can read from this citation that Sara wonders whether she had fallen prey to "the Jewish chic," whether her own Jewishness is not or was not just another case of following the "Jewish fashion." She has been an active member of the Warsaw community for more than fifteen years now, and her own usage of the past tense suggests that her "self-suspicions" no longer "haunt" her. The following is another sentence from the interview, this time in the present tense.

> I feel authentic in that I doubt, in that uncertainty about who I am, about whether I am connected, whether I have the right to this tradition. (Sara)

It is striking how Sara seems to identify doubt and self-questioning with authenticity. In a prominently existential remark, she becomes an advocate of a particular understanding of identity, which sees it as unstable (not fixed), and a particular understanding of authenticity, which assumes an instability of identity (Charmé 2000). I mentioned Sartre (1948) earlier with his idea of authenticity, which carries an "ontological insecurity" and is beyond that which is fixed and established. Charmé paraphrases the French philosopher and concludes that what makes Jewish identity an authentic one is the assumption of the instability of all identities (Sartre 1948; Charmé 2000).

Sara also mentions the idea of having (or not having) "the right" to "this tradition," that is, to Judaism or Jewishness. A similar question appeared in my interview with Wiktor.

> Can I allow myself to call myself a Jew-Jew, if because of deepest cultural assimilation I was totally deprived of that culture, raised in a Polish home . . . ? (Wiktor)

The important observation here is that none of the participants were actually raised to be Jewish, nobody actively transmitted Jewish tradition to them, and nobody expected them to embrace Jewish culture. None of them can be called a "Jew-Jew"—a Jew born and raised as a Jew, as it seems to be defined by Wiktor. Consequently, when entering any area of Jewish life they have to confront their own sense of unfamiliarity; they have to confront lack of knowledge of Jewish tradition and lack of any "practical" Jewish background. In a similar tone, Magda complains about not being "equipped" with the right "tools" to be Jewish, in the practical sense.

> How am I supposed to know Jewish prayers if in my home nobody ever prayed in the Jewish way? How am I supposed to know what is what if I never saw the things before in my life? (Magda)

Later on she adds,

> I'd like to learn Hebrew, but then again I'm not sure if that isn't trying to fill up my identity with something external. (Magda)

Here, Magda admits that beyond the feeling of inadequacy due to "Jewish illiteracy," there is that existential void, that existential inadequacy, which, as I believe she suggests, cannot be fixed by Hebrew lessons.

> I regret I was never that annoying Jewish kid who dis-
> turbs everyone in the synagogue and who never had to
> learn the difference between the Torah and the Talmud
> . . . (Ewelina)

Ewelina regrets never having the opportunity to be a Jewish child, who knows the difference between the Torah and the Talmud "by osmosis," by the sole fact of being raised in an awareness of "Jewish things." Today, Ewelina obviously knows the difference between the two. She wishes, however, for that difference to be a self-evident one for her, one she would have naturally been raised with. Her personal Jewishness begins in early adulthood, and it "misses" its childhood. The existential void, if I may call it that, is not in not knowing the difference between the Torah and the Talmud, it is in never having been a Jewish child. In longing for a Jewish childhood, Ewelina in fact expresses a longing for a personal Jewish past—one that she could remember as her very own. Such personal Jewish pasts are missing from the experience of the third post-Holocaust generation of Jews in Poland—yet another profoundly influential common denominator.

In a slightly more bitter tone, Bożena also describes the feeling of being deprived of a Jewish background, and of a Jewish upbringing.

> My Jews didn't wait for me. They didn't survive. I feel
> betrayed. I was taught to love Warszawa [Warsaw], but
> where is my Varshe [Warsaw in Yiddish]? (Bożena)

She blames history for having deprived her of personal Jewish history. She blames it for the fact that she could not inherit the memory of a Jewish Warsaw. She was taught how to be Polish but not how to be Jewish. Bożena goes on to say,

> I consider myself a Polish Jew because it is my iden-
> tity—that I am a Polish Jew and that we are no more.
> This is why I am a miserable orphan. I looked for those
> Jews who were taken from me by the war. I waited and
> searched for them, as if they could come back. (Bożena).

The idea of being orphaned was also mentioned by Teresa. In addition, further in the interview, Teresa brought up the notion of being homeless.

> My home was taken away from me, and I will never find
> it again. (Teresa)

What we can see here is an assortment of feelings of being betrayed, orphaned, homeless, or abandoned. Another interesting statement in this context is that of Marek, who I quoted earlier in a larger fragment.

> I embraced an identity that isn't there. (Marek)

This idea of embracing an identity which does not exist can be understood as embracing a potential identity—one that would have been available in an alternative scenario of history. In other words, the individual "complaints" here are that things were not meant to be this way, that Jews were not meant to disappear from Poland, and that things could have been "normal" for the young generation. The somewhat abstract feeling of mission or of owing something to history, which I described earlier, turns out to be accompanied by a feeling of being betrayed by that same history. This sense of being betrayed by history is followed by "what if" type of thinking, and it provides some form of rationale for being Jewish, in a place where Jews used to flourish and then virtually disappeared. The idea then is to be Jewish *as if* history had not severed Jewish ancestries. The narratives indeed brought up the question of what would happen had history unraveled completely differently—had there been no Holocaust, no World War II, no persecutions, and no communism. This "what if . . ." nostalgia presents itself as an actual part of the participants' Jewish narratives—as something that immediately followed the discovery of Jewish roots. In other words, in some cases, we may argue that embracing Jewish identity is in fact an act of reclaiming an identity that "could have been" theirs (I shall discuss this further in the discussion and conclusions section). And in this sense, it is one of the ways in which they seem to explain the fact that they pursue being Jewish. This is also represented in the following citations:

> If it weren't for persecutions and antisemitism, I think

my family would be totally Jewish and I wouldn't have to struggle what to do in order to live a normal life without any problems. (Natalia)

To discover that which could have been if it weren't for . . . How I could have turned out if someone back there hadn't converted to Christianity, hadn't chosen the assimilationist way. (Wiktor)

. . . I would like to be part of that world, the one I would surely have belonged to from the beginning if it weren't for the Second World War. And it would have been a completely Jewish world, perhaps not super religious, maybe even totally secular, but it would be that very world . . . (Hana)

These examples seem to talk about an idea of alternative lives. In other words, Natalia and Wiktor, for example, appear to struggle today for a way of life which could have naturally been "theirs," if history had allowed it. In the discussion and conclusions section, I shall devote more attention to such discourse and I will show how it can be compared with the narratives of adoptees.

In the following citations, we encounter the idea of having been deprived of the world of Polish Jewry from before its destruction. Interestingly, as we can see in the third example, "that world" can also be associated with the ghetto.

As I began identifying with it, I felt that this world, my world, was totally taken away from me. (Teresa)

I never knew it. I miss that [world] in Poland before the war so much. (Natalia)

I would give twenty years of my life to be able to go to the ghetto for just a moment, I mean to the ghetto for Shabbat at my grandparents', to know exactly what the atmosphere was, what they talked about, what they ate, how they behaved, how they looked at each other, how they talked to each other, just to know that. (Sara)

I come back to the discussion of the individual sense of authenticity in the section about models of self-authentication.

Sense of Authenticity vis-à-vis Others

> There are those who feel more Jewish, those who feel less Jewish, and those who take away from others that right to feel anybody at all. (Anabela)

The previous citation can be a good motto for this section, which tackles with the participants' accounts of the experiences of facing manifold accusations of inauthenticity. My interviewees talked extensively about the different ways in which other people question their Jewishness and tell them that they are not "real" Jews. This first type of questioning is considered with the ethnic label, with whether a given person is *Jewish enough*, in the "biological" sense. The chief criterion here is always the criterion of Orthodox halacha, with its definition of a Jew as someone descended from a Jewish mother. For the most part, this type of questioning does not affect those who have a Jewish mother and can provide substantial "evidence" of it. The other type of questioning my interviewees experience is when certain people question their choice to pursue a Jewish identity relatively late in life, and in a country like Poland. The latter involves the assumption that Poland is fiercely antisemitic and nothing beyond a vast Jewish graveyard, which continues to be a popular opinion among Jews outside Poland.

These two different types of questioning are used by three groups of "other people." The "others" my interviewees mention are as follows:

1.   Foreign Jews (generally American and Israeli Jews)
2.   Non-Jewish Poles
3.   Other Young Polish Jews

The two types of questioning can be represented by such model questions or accusations:

1. *But you're not really Jewish!*
2. *Why would you suddenly want to be Jewish, let alone in Poland?!*

The first type of questioning appears, as reported by my interviewees, on the part of all three groups. The second type appears most commonly on the part of the first group (foreign Jews), and I have no record of it being used by either non-Jewish Poles or by other young Polish Jews.

Being Questioned by Foreign Jews:
But You're Not Really Jewish!

Odelia describes having been in a relationship with a foreign Jew who eventually said he would not marry her because she was not "halachically Jewish." Odelia has a Jewish father.

> It's a sad rule, that you're only Jewish after the mother,
> so my children won't be Jewish even if I marry a Jew . . .
> If I meet a man, who will only see a Jewess in me after I
> convert, that wouldn't be fair. (Odelia)

She recalls the story of how her relationship ended because she was not recognized as Jewish by her boyfriend as a "slap in the face"; she says if she feels Jewish, then "what right does he have" to judge her in this way.

Aleksandra mentions the fact that there are people whose first question for her is always "Are you Jewish?" Her statement relates to American Jews, which is clear from the context as well as from the fact that she quotes the "Are you Jewish?" question in the original English.

> 'Are you Jewish?' . . . You know . . . for them it's the first
> thing—it's after the mother that you are Jewish, it's always like this . . . (Aleksandra)

Sara mentions a similar circumstance with regard to Israelis. She says the attitude changes right away as soon as people learn that only her father was Jewish and not her mother.

> Someone invites you for Shabbat and changes their attitude right after you tell them . . . (Sara)

In the following example, Bożena mentions both Americans and Israelis.

> As a Polish Jew I didn't feel recognized or respected enough by American institutions and of course not by Israeli institutions . . . it was as if we were second-quality Jews. (Bożena)

Some interviewees also resort to the argument that had they been born before World War II, they would not have to debate their own Jewishness. In other words, they tend to emphasize that they would qualify as Jews according to Nazi laws. This is exemplified in the following quote.

> If someone falls under the Nuremberg Laws, then he is Jewish for me. (Jadwiga)

To sum up, in this category we can see examples of foreign Jews questioning young Polish Jews' authenticity as Jews. Evidently, there is no such thing, according to the Jewish law in its Orthodox version, as a "non-halachic Jew." Ironically though, more than half of the young Jews in today's Poland are "non-halachic Jews." This is a phenomenon whose significance cannot be overestimated. The processes of assimilation among Jews worldwide can be held responsible for the existence of individual "non-halachic Jews," but I would argue that what is responsible for the existence of an entire community of "non-halachic Jews" (as is the case with young Polish Jews today) is the contemporary process of "de-assimilation." I shall explain this further in the discussion and conclusions section.

Being Questioned by Foreign Jews:
Why Would You Suddenly Want to Be Jewish, Let Alone in Poland?!

The narratives have shown that there is a general sense of frustration with the opinion other Jews (American and Israeli Jews in particular) have about Jewish life in Poland or the "lack thereof." The insensitive attitude of foreign Jews in their interaction with the Polish Jewish community is mentioned by Rosenson (2003). She distinguishes three outside opinions, as they are reported by her interviewees. The first one is that Polish Jewish culture died irreversibly with the Holocaust. The second is that Jewish identity in Poland must be limited to dealing with what is believed to be raging Polish antisemitism. The third argument mentioned by Rosenson is that because of the Holocaust and Polish antisemitism, Jewish life in Poland is impossible, and therefore those who see themselves as Jewish and remain in Poland are in fact not "real" Jews (Rosenson 2003). The chief predicament here seems to be that the idea of being Jewish in Poland after the war has fallen prey to stereo-typization, misunderstandings, and sheer disbelief. In the interviews I conducted, the participants refer to American or Israeli Jews' attitudes toward Jewish life in Poland, and the types of opinions mentioned are fairly parallel to those discussed by Rosenson. The reason American and Israeli Jews are mentioned is naturally because they are the two groups of Jews who visit Poland most commonly and come into contact with its young Polish Jewish population. Many of the participants have had the opportunity to meet some of those who come on "root trips," or "Holocaust trips" to Poland, and in some cases they recall interact-ing with Israeli and American Jews while in Israel. Furthermore, the American and Israeli Jewish communities are the world's largest and best-established Jewish communities—this only deepens the striking disproportion between them and the Polish community as well as the common misconceptions which occur on the part of American and Israeli Jews with regard to Poland and its Jews.

> I want to show them [American and Israeli Jews] that we exist and that we are human beings and that we have a lot to say about our struggle with discontinuity of Polish Jewish community and about our disconnectedness from the entire Jewish world. (Bożena)

Bożena expresses a strong feeling of not being acknowledged by other Jews as part of an existing community. She also talks about how Polish Jews do not have the opportunity to try to explain to other Jews what sort of a challenge it is to be Jewish in Poland. The "disconnectedness" she mentions is seen as resulting from a lack of proper communication with other Jews.

> According to Jews in the United States and in Israel, there are no Jews in Poland, and that is a huge problem, because . . . those groups come here, and they look at you like you're a monkey in a zoo and "what do you mean you found out that you're Jewish when you were 15?!" But we should talk about this, so that they have an awareness of this . . . It pisses me off when Israelis say, "How can you live in this huge cemetery?" . . . and so on, but I think it's important for Jews to live in Poland. (Joanna)

This expresses a feeling of not being recognized or understood by American and Israeli Jews. According to Joanna and many others, foreign Jews cannot seem to grasp how one can suddenly find out that they are Jewish and, worse yet, pursue being Jewish in a country like Poland. It seems that young Jews in Poland are in fact accused of being "strange." More irritation with regard to this is expressed in the following citation.

> The Israeli trips come here and pay to see the Holocaust . . . they build this propaganda . . . (Ewelina)

The experience of having to actively confront the Israeli attitude to Jewish life in Poland is best reflected in the following fragment.

> [They ask me] "How can you live in a country where three million Jews were killed?" And then I say: This is my country, this is where I was born, this is where my family is, so what do you want me to do? Go to Israel? "Yes!" So I say "This is my country and my mission . . .

Jews living in the Diaspora is also a solution." I educate in this way, this whole propaganda drives me nuts, I feel like there is something I should do about this, that these people need to be educated. (Odelia)

Many participants feel this strongly about what some of them have defined as Israeli "chutzpah." This may be because Poles are especially sensitive to propaganda. The communist experience, even if not immediate, is such a strong factor in identifying political or ideological phenomena that it is true that Israelis have a hard time convincing young Poles that the State of Israel is a perfect country. Eleven of my participants made a point of this during the interviews. Importantly, all of the participants in this study have indicated their sympathy for Israel, including several who would identify as Zionist. However, many of them nevertheless criticized Israelis for their use of ideological propaganda and often for being unfairly biased in their opinions about Poland and Polish Jews. In the following citation, Ewelina remembers her visit in Israel:

> They put on this Zionist show, which had very clear connotations for people from Poland, it sounded like proper propaganda . . . I really didn't like it, but the Americans . . . I think they received it better, for them it was actually neat, you know . . ."community" and all . . . (Ewelina)

Once again, we can detect sarcasm here, which is so characteristic of our population. Magda also visited Israel on a Birthright trip, and her comments very much resemble those of Ewelina.

> Maybe it's because we come from this part of the world, where history was what it was and associations with propaganda are unequivocal . . . This does not change the fact that all those Americans are convinced that it's right and they buy it. (Magda)

Again, we can see a tendency to criticize Israelis for being obnoxious and Americans for being naive. In my interview with Magda, she went on to also criticize the Israeli groups which visit Poland. The following comes from Ewelina.

> It's like this: they come here to the sad and ugly Poland, where the earth is soaked with Jewish blood . . . and then you go to Eretz [Israel] and you can see life! (Ewelina)

What Ewelina is referring to is "March of the Living"—an annual program that brings students from around the world to march from Auschwitz to Birkenau in memory of the victims of the Holocaust. After a few days in Poland, most participants travel on to Israel, where they celebrate the Israeli Independence Day. The March was primarily designed as a study in contrasts. Established in 1988, it has over the years rewritten its mission to include some interaction with the Polish and the Polish Jewish community. Together with several participants in this study, I participated in March of the Living in 2002. As Polish Jewish students, we were not allowed to make a public address and were actively discouraged (with the help of security officers) from interacting with the students from other countries who marched along with us. All this was in an attempt to protect the powerful message of the March that Poland was the site of nothing but antisemitism and annihilation, whereas Israel was the only desirable site of Jewish life after the Holocaust.

I must note once again that despite certain critical remarks about Israeli Zionist propaganda and in a number of cases about right-wing Israeli politics, all of the interviewees struck me as decidedly pro-Israeli. In fact, criticizing Israel is generally part of the internal communal discourse—it is something the participants are likely to do between themselves. Nevertheless, in discussions with non-Jews, they are determined to defend Israel. This is expressed in quite straightforward statements such as

> In Israel I have to defend Poland and in Poland I have to defend Israel. (. . .) I'm a Polish patriot in many ways. I'm sick of Israelis being so anti-Polish and so ignorant. (Bożena)

Max reflects in a similar way:

> In Israel I say that I'm Polish. In every country except
> Poland I say I'm Polish. In Poland I say I'm a Jew. It's
> significant. (Max)

Being Questioned by Non-Jewish Poles:
But You're Not Really Jewish!

For non-Jewish Poles, the dominant Orthodox notion of Jewish ancestral law, which defines a person as Jewish if he or she was born to
a Jewish mother, is generally a well-known fact. I can say this on the
basis of years of experience with Poles from different strata of society.
Although it is not difficult in Poland to meet someone who does not
know that Shabbat begins on Friday night, I have not encountered
anybody who never heard that Jewishness is inherited after the
mother. The participants in my study who do not have Jewish mothers
(whether they converted to Judaism or not) often report being "accused" by Poles of not being Jewish at all or of being some sort of
"fake" Jews.

The way Franka puts it is that "even Poles" would say to her that she
is not Jewish at all if she does not have a Jewish mother but only a
Jewish father. Wiktor mentions encountering the same problem.

> A regular Pole asks me "But who is your mother?" and
> I say "A Polish Catholic." "So you're not Jewish!" Such a
> person, who has no right at all to judge me . . . in the eyes
> of a complete goy I am disqualified as a Jew, because ac-
> cidentally he knows this much [that a Jew ought to have
> a Jewish mother]. (Wiktor)

Wiktor has a Jewish father. We can observe here the peculiar conflict reflected in his discourse. Wiktor talks about a "regular Pole,"
perhaps because he himself is a Pole, although not a "regular" one.
Moreover, he labels the person who confronts him a "complete goy." Is
the assumption here that he himself is a goy (according to Orthodox

halacha) but not a "complete" one (based on his primordial "blood-link")? Allow me to address the issue further in the discussion and conclusions section.

Jewish law—the halacha—in its Orthodox interpretation determines that a person is Jewish if his or her mother is Jewish, or if they underwent religious conversion to Judaism, recognized by the Orthodox rabbinate. The halachic criterion of descent turned out to provide the most common problem in our context of authenticity. Because most of the participants do not have Jewish mothers, their narratives include numerous examples of being accused of not being real Jews, or of not being recognized as full-fledged Jews. Not in every case is it actually clear who the particular interviewee is referring to when he or she talks about "others" or "people." We can see this in the following examples.

> I don't have a Jewish mother, but I don't like to be called a non-Jew. (Marek)

> And so "goy" turns out to be the insult, not "Jew" anymore, but "goy." (Stella)

> Every situation in which someone tells me that I'm not a Jew is very hard, it devastates me, it destroys everything that I had managed to work out for myself, that identity, that sense of identity. (Łukasz)

Here, Łukasz describes how other people repeatedly attack and "destroy" his identity. Łukasz has a Jewish father. He underwent circumcision several years ago but has not undergone a full Orthodox conversion

One more example of questioning the authenticity of our participants by non-Jewish Poles is mentioned by Alex. He complains about the tendency to stereotype with regard to Jews.

> The Jewish Culture Festival in Krakow is very typical with regard to the Polish attitude to Jewish themes, that is the growing conviction of many Poles in metropolitan areas that Jewishness and Jewish culture are "cool," but what they have in mind is a Jewish culture in the form

of Fiddler on the Roof or Galician Klezmer bands. And so when you mention Jewish roots, the image they [the Poles] have in front of them has nothing to do with the life of young Polish Jews, and to some extent people are shocked that one can be a young Polish Jew and not have sidelocks and be a regular young person. (Alex)

Alex describes the feeling of not fitting the stereotype. His frustration is directed at the fact that there may be a level of ignorance with regard to Jews among some crowds in Poland, even the ones attracted to "Jewish things." Iris Weiss uses the term "Jewish Disneyland" to describe the phenomenon, and notes that "Real Jews, insofar as they are still around, cannot match the fictional image. They are therefore a disappointment" (Weiss 2002). Ruth Ellen Gruber notes how there is a blurry line between "manifestations that deal with Jews and Jewish culture as living entities and those that treat, and sometimes separate them as an isolated, exotic, or even codified category" (Gruber 2009). In defense of the Jewish Culture Festival in Krakow which Alex refers to, it must be said that it has consciously tried to move beyond the idealized *Fiddler on the Roof* aesthetic despite that aesthetic being much coveted by the Festival's Polish audience. The input of Jewish artists and intellectuals from all over the world, as well as from Poland, together with an emphasis on high artistic quality and the *genius loci of* Krakow's Jewish district of Kazimierz, accounts for the Festival's uniqueness among other European venues of this kind (Makuch 2009). Finally, in presenting a more and more diversified image of Jewish culture, it may in fact begin to contribute to the process of breaking away from some of the stereotypes which exist in Poland with regard to Jews.

Being Questioned by Other Young Polish Jews:
But You're Not Really Jewish!

I showed earlier that the members of the third post-Holocaust generation of Jews in Poland question themselves in a number of ways. The following are examples of how they question each other.

The first context where I have encountered accounts of an individual being questioned by other members of the group is the context of Jewish denominations. The majority of acting Jewish congregations in Poland are officially Orthodox, with the exception of small Reform congregations in Warsaw and Krakow. Among my interviewees, eight have been or still are associated with Warsaw's Reform congregation.

The following is a citation from one of the members of the Reform community of Warsaw:

> On Twarda, what counts most is whether you're halachic or not, because if you're not halachic you don't count at all. (Anabela)

Anabela describes here the "rules" on Twarda Street, where the Orthodox Jewish Congregation in Warsaw has its premises. Although it is possible to be a member of the Orthodox community of Warsaw as a "non-halachic Jew," what Anabela points out is that on Twarda, having a Jewish father is not enough for everyone to recognize her as a legitimate Jew. She feels that there are other Polish Jews who question her own Jewishness. At the same time, she mentions feeling more at ease at the Reform congregation, where everybody is new, and where people who have a Jewish father are not less appreciated as Jews. A similar reflection appeared in my interview with Magda. She too prefers the Reform community over the Orthodox one and justifies it in the following way:

> There [at the Reform Congregation center], anybody can come and they have every right to feel displaced at the beginning . . . , and to not know much, because how are they supposed to know . . . (Magda)

What Magda points out, as she continues, is that some Orthodox Jews in Warsaw look down upon the Reform. Interestingly, the issue this poses for Magda is not that of not being Jewish enough, because she happens to be one of the few young people in Warsaw who have two Jewish parents. However, as in the previous citation, most people at the Reform community center are not "halachic Jews" in the eyes of the mainstream Orthodox. Hence, people who associate themselves with the Reform are exposed to a twofold "authenticity check": on the one hand, they are questioned with regard to their Jewish roots, that is, they are questioned as to whether they are Jewish enough; on the other hand, the question is whether they are "good Jews." The latter brings up the question of whether one can be an authentic "good" Reform Jew.

Let me mention another example of being questioned with regard to non-halachic roots. Robert, who is a child of a Jewish father and a non-Jewish mother, describes the authenticity problem in a more abstract perspective. It is also only from the context that we can tell that the "people" he talks about are some of his Polish Jewish friends.

> I would prefer to be halachic, because there are people who have a problem with me . . . (Robert)

Interestingly, three of Robert's four grandparents were Jewish. It so happens that his mother's mother is not Jewish. His own comment is that it can be considered "bad luck." His "roots situation," if I may, is very peculiar and indeed not very common in Poland. From participant observation, I have learned that his circumstance is often brought up in discussions among the representatives of the generation. His mere existence seems to challenge general assumptions about Jewish identity. Interestingly, his looks are also commonly brought up by many as an excellent example of "Jewish looks," whatever these may be. Still, as Robert mentions, some of his peers would call him a non-Jew. Indeed, the "game" of "Who is more Jewish?" is a dangerous one to play among the representatives of the "unexpected generation."

Greg complains about the phenomenon in the following way.

> Yes, [it's about] survival . . . but calling each other non-Jew names is totally stupid, because if someone feels Jewish then he has his reasons, and you cannot take that from anyone. (Greg)

Beside citations, where the questions about authenticity came from an identifiable group of people, I might like to mention some of those, where the "others" referred to are not specified, but they appear to be either one or all of the groups at once.

> Nobody has the right to tell me that I am not Jewish . . .

I think only stupid people judge others. (Franka)

Here, the citation is already an expression of self-defense in reaction to anybody who attempts to tell our Franka, whose father is Jewish, that she is not Jewish. Aleksandra reports that there are people out there who think that everything she does in terms of her Jewish life is "some kind of madness." Their opinion does not stop her from doing her "mad things." She too has a Jewish father. Aleksandra adds another remark.

> I do something and it is authentic, I want it to be au-
> thentic, I make an effort, and it meets my needs. And
> whether somebody understands it or not is their prob-
> lem. (Aleksandra)

In the previous statement, our participant expresses that she understands the fact that some people fail to appreciate her or what she does. Similarly, Sara says that, in reality, everyone can question her "and people do actually do that." I will mention more examples of being questioned when I present my material about conversion to Judaism.

The "Real" Jew

Another aspect of the discussion of authenticity is revealed in my interviewees' individual opinions about what is perceived to be an "abstract authentic Jewishness" and about what is perceived as "real Jewishness" outside the Polish context.

It is important to note here that all participants made references to authenticity. However, most of those references were made in one of the contexts mentioned earlier: the context of the young Polish Jewish community and the particular individual contexts. Examples of citations referring to a more abstract idea of authenticity or more specifically to "authentic Jewishness" are fewer. However, they prove useful as they appear in juxtaposition to individual renderings of the "uniqueness" of being Jewish in Poland.

Third-generation Jews in Poland have different ideas of what it takes to be an authentic Jew as part of the Jewish collective, which is multigenerational and communally organized (unlike the Polish context). The most common references made here are to American and Israeli Jewish communities, which are perceived to be precisely what the Polish Jewish community is not: "large," "strong," "defined," and "normal."

One of the components of the perceived "real Jewishness" is religious Orthodoxy. Although only ten of our participants are observant Jews, as many as eighteen state that they prefer Orthodox Judaism over liberal movements. Here are some examples of such statements.

> [Orthodoxy] is something that comes from roots, it derives from history. Orthodox religion has been there for centuries . . . it is inscribed in tradition. (Odelia)

Odelia herself is not religious, although she sometimes attends activities at the Orthodox Congregation as well as the Reform Congregation in Warsaw. In contrast, the following citation comes from Danuta, who has a Jewish father. She converted to Modern Orthodox Judaism but lives a relatively liberal Jewish life.

> I'm interested in the traditional form of Judaism, I don't know why . . . I think . . . for me . . . it is more original in the sense of being most authentic. (Danuta)

In a similar essentializing tone, Marek talks about his preferences in types of Judaism.

> Orthodoxy seems most Jewish to me. If you're going to be religious, then be religious, and not in the middle. (Marek)

Marek is not recognized as Jewish by Orthodox halacha. He was circumcised a few years ago but has not decided to undergo full conversion as of yet.

There is another aspect which is mentioned as a requirement for being a "normal," "authentic," or "real" Jew. Namely, "authentic" Jewishness is perceived as an "unchallenged" or "secure" one. This is understood as resulting from having been born Jewish and brought up Jewish, as opposed to having been born Polish and "converted" or "transitioned" into being

Jewish. It is best represented in the following citation.

> Authentic Jewishness is . . . wondering what it's really like
> to be a goy . . . it's the kind of Jewishness, which doesn't
> ask itself whether or not it is Jewish. (Sara)

In the interview, Sara admits that within such a definition of authentic Jewishness, she does not come across as an authentic Jew herself. She admits that although she associates this sense of certainty of Jewish identity with being authentic (in general), she herself feels authentic in her own uncertainty (in particular). I return to this excerpt once more.

> I feel authentic . . . in that uncertainty about who I am . . .
> (Sara)

The contradictions that transpire in Sara's narrative illustrate some of the fundamental characteristics of the identities of "the unexpected generation"—their "uncertainty," their never-ending process of becoming, necessarily accompanied by self-questioning.

MODELS OF SELF-AUTHENTICATION

Conversion

THE PROCESS OF ESTABLISHING an individual sense of authenticity is necessarily contextualized, and it must be appreciated that the participants' construction of their sense of authenticity grows out of interaction with the outside world. In other words, self-questioning is necessarily a product of dialogic interaction with other people, and it takes place within a framework of prevailing social and cultural representations and discourses (Billig 1993; Harré and Gillett 1995). Here is where different models of self-authentication come to play.

When it comes to authenticating oneself vis-à-vis the Jewish community, conversion becomes the main model of authentication. Whether or not the individuals actually decide to undergo the process, conversion has become a very significant element in the Polish Jewish narrative as a means of expressing one's perception of cultural boundaries.

In many instances, conversion is referred to as a form of strategy. Clearly, it is a strategy many choose not to resort to. Nevertheless, it is an immanent element of the discourse on Jewish identity among young Jewish adults in Poland. Whether or not one decides to undergo conversion, it constitutes a point of reference in the processes of self-defining as well as in determining the boundaries of Jewish belonging. The first context I want to present here is that in which conversion is mentioned by the participants as a possibility, as a type of strategy of entering the Jewish community as a full-fledged member.

Let me present two stories of conversion: that of Danuta, who converted under Modern Orthodox auspices in Poland, and that of Bożena, who converted in Israel under Conservative auspices.

Danuta was baptized and raised in a practicing Catholic home. In her teens, she found out that her father was not her biological father. It turned out that the latter was alive, abroad . . . and Jewish. She met him, but they do not maintain a close relationship. Nevertheless, discovering that she had Jewish roots was a breakthrough for Danuta. She says that even before she knew her biological father was Jewish, she felt "an inclination" to study Judaism. After she found out, she met "a whole bunch" of other people like herself, and when she first entered the Warsaw synagogue, she "got a strong kick," and "it was the first thing" in her life she "was ready to fight for." She says she wondered for some time whether it was a good idea to change so much in adult life, whether it made sense at all, but she "couldn't give it up"—it was too important. One day she woke up—she says—and realized that she could no longer live a different life. She just "had to" be Jewish. She admits that she did feel a bit rejected by some because her mother was not Jewish, and so she did have the thought "somewhere in the back of her head" that she would be "treated better" by some after she converted. Neither of her parents was thrilled about her decision to pursue Jewishness. She says she chose Orthodoxy because she perceives it to be the "original" form of Judaism in the sense of being the most "authentic" one. Today, she calls herself a Polish Jewess. She believes a "Jewish soul" had been lost and was then recovered in her. Before she discovered her Jewish connection, she "had no idea who she was," but now she knows who she is, how she wants her life to turn out, and what she believes in, and it gives her "strength and stability in life." Nevertheless, Danuta admits that what accompanied her conversion process was "a lot of stress," "pain," and feelings of "not being accepted," and "injustice." She adds a cynical note about possible future family life.

> I'm aware of the fact that I'll get married, and my moth-
> er-in-law will continue to make my life miserable until
> she dies.

She appears to accept the fact that there will always be people who may never accept her. Danuta concludes the story of her conversion and of her pursuit of Jewishness with these words:

> I am someone who chose Judaism, but I'm not sure if
> it's not some kind of ideology, which I add onto it now

to legitimize my being Jewish . . . I think, referring to those souls at Sinai, that it was predetermined . . . So it was hidden somewhere inside me, and it was just meant to be.

Let me recap now the second story of conversion to Judaism. Like Danuta, Bożena was baptized, but the household she grew up in was not very Catholic in terms of religious practice. Growing up, Bożena had a Polish Catholic mother and a secular Jewish father. She only really realized that she was of Jewish origin when she was in high school. When she started to identify with Jewishness, her parents were not thrilled. Nevertheless, Bożena became one of the most important young Jewish activists in Poland; she became chief editor of a Jewish magazine and was active in the Polish Union of Jewish Students. She decided to undergo conversion after emigrating to Israel. She began the process under the Orthodox auspices but soon decided to switch to the Conservative movement's conversion process, which she eventually completed. She describes converting as "painful."

No one and nothing can ever try to take away from me my grandma, my Warsaw, or myself. Conversion never meant for me to become Jewish. It was accomplishing some kind of religious process. And a bit to dance as they play.

Bożena says "her Jews" never made it, they "didn't wait" for her; therefore, she has to "deal with" the ones that are available now, and "they have their shortcomings."

I dance to their music because I want to dance with them. And I learn it better and faster than they would ever learn one seed of the truth.

What is the truth Bożena is referring to which she is convinced will never be understood by some people? Perhaps, as the rest of the interview undoubtedly suggests, she is referring to the unique and untranslatable Polish Jewish experience.

The decision to convert was never a decision to become
Jewish. I was Jewish long before that.

Bożena had recognized herself as Jewish at a time when most people
around her were unwilling to do so. "Dancing to their music" meant a
compromise—she decided to conform to the expectations of the particular society she wanted to be part of. There is a sense of bitterness
that lingers on.

She is very dissatisfied with the Orthodox approach to conversion.
They make a circus of it, she says. Although she lives a relatively observant Jewish life, she criticizes Orthodox Judaism for the simple reason
that "they make you wear skirts." As far as being recognized by other
Jews (American and Israeli), she feels they view people like her as "second quality" Jews.

There are a number of similarities in the two stories: both women
were raised quite unaware of their Jewish roots and both get their
Jewish roots from the father. Both decided to pursue a Jewish identity,
became active in the Jewish community, and chose a level of Jewish religious observance. It is also true that both wanted to convert Orthodox.
So the first difference is that in the end Bożena converted Conservative.
But the fact is that the differences are not very significant. Neither one
of the interviewees talks about her conversion as a joyful or satisfying
experience. In both cases it is described as something they simply "had
to do" because of certain social expectations. Hence, conversion was not
meant to grant them Jewishness but rather a better status in the global
Jewish community. Both accounts mention a feeling of things being
unfair. First, the individual efforts to be Jewish are not appreciated by
the rest of the Jewish world. Second, conversion does not actually guarantee that one will be treated as a legitimate Jew anywhere one goes.
As is the case for many members of our population, Danuta and Bożena
made serious changes in their lives and became Jewish, only to be told
that they were not Jewish at all; they then converted in order to be more
"officially" Jewish, only to find out that for some they will never be as
Jewish as the "really Jewish Jews."

The fact is that only fourteen of our participants are certain that
their mothers are Jewish. Hence, the problem of not being "real," "authentic," or "Jewish enough" is relevant for as many as thirty-six of the
interviewees. As a matter of fact, the problem is also present in the

accounts of the "halachically Jewish" participants.

Aneta believes that her mother is Jewish but has found no way to prove it. She says she considered conversion but decided against it because she did not plan to become religious.

> It did bother me that I wasn't undergoing conversion, that I would be . . . somehow sociologically speaking an outcast, that I wouldn't be seen as . . . a member of the world Jewish population. (Aneta)

She seems to accept, for the time being, that with her current "roots status," she cannot fully belong. Odelia brings up another aspect of being a "non-halachic Jew" (she has a Jewish father). She relates her potential decision to convert to her family status.

> Possibly, if I was with a Jew for real, I would convert for my kids, so that they would be Jews, would be recognized as Jews. (Odelia)

We can see here that although she does not seek immediate self-authentication in the form of conversion for herself, she already considers "authenticating" her future children. Franka states clearly that others' attitudes do affect her thoughts about potential conversion.

> I have to admit that [through converting] I would get rid of a few problems like who I really am . . . maybe finally my friends would see me as a Jew (Franka)

Eryk also talks about how he is perceived by the outside world. In the following quote, he is referring to the Israeli rabbinic law, in whose light he would not be considered Jewish, although he is eligible for immigration.

> I wouldn't want to be a second quality citizen, so to speak. Only in this sense I'd want to do it, in order to fix my status. I don't need it for my identity, but it would make my life easier (Eryk).

In fact, later in the interview Eryk shared with me what really pushes him to consider conversion (as I mentioned earlier, Eryk underwent circumcision but has not yet made the final decision with regard to conversion).

> In the Orthodox version of Judaism there is a problem with pouring wine. Only a halachic person is allowed to pour wine. If a non-halachic person pours wine it is de-koshered and a halachic person cannot drink it. This creates some conflicts during parties. If someone already brings kosher wine, what do we do with it, who should pour it . . . And somehow it really bothered me . . . because there is this friend, I myself pulled him into this whole Jewishness, he's halachic, he happens to be a Jew, well he feels Jewish but not quite, he doesn't take it [as seriously] as I do, for him it's less big of a deal. And he's [considered] more Jewish than me and he can pour that wine. And that just pisses me off. So it's this drop, this drop of wine, which determines that I have to convert. So that I can have the patent for pouring wine at parties. (Eryk)

Eryk's case shows very well that conversion presents itself as a strategy of changing one's status within the community. In this sense, it appears to be more of a social than a religious phenomenon in our context. None of the individuals cited above is religiously observant. They all consider themselves Jewish, but secular. As I mentioned earlier, very few young Polish Jews choose to live an observant Jewish life. Such is the case with both the "halachic" and the "non-halachic" ones. The problem the latter often mention is that in their case converting would in fact be an "act of inauthenticity." This is how Wiktor explains why he chooses not to convert.

> I wouldn't want to convert just so that I could get a cer-tificate—that I'm OK . . . and then after conversion quit religion, because that would be a lie. (Wiktor)

Wiktor admits that converting would in fact grant him some kind of legitimization of his Jewishness, but because he knows that he is not religious, he thinks it would be "cheating" to convert *pro forma*. It would be an "inauthentic authentication," if you like. Similarly, Ewelina recalls considering conversion in the past.

> Some two years ago I had this crazy idea, that in fact maybe it would be cool to convert, I mean to become more Jewish and all . . . (Ewelina)

She eventually decided against converting because being religious—as she phrased it—"it's not the kind of lifestyle" for her. An interesting reflection was formulated by Iris, who believes tradition is crucial to Jewish identity, yet does not consider herself religious at this point.

> Is it a matter of recognition or of some people's opinions, or is it a matter of what is inside of you? If it [Jewishness] is in you and it is true and natural then you don't have the need to tell and show others that you have it, be-cause it is in accordance with you, and you don't need the environment to confirm it for you. That is the basic rule, because if it is in you and you really feel it, then you don't need what the others think . . . You just are it. (Iris)

The next category of references to conversion in the context of au-thenticity is one in which the participants who did undergo conversion give accounts of what their conversion changed, with regard to being recognized by others as Jews. The prevalent attitude is reflected in the citations, which show that the participants "complain" about conversion not being as effective a mode of authentication as they would expect it to be. In other words, they say that although they converted, there are still people who fail to accept them as legitimate Jews. As an example, Sara says that after conversion she was often "called names."

> "Goy," "antisemite," "convert" . . . and these allusions that we accept some Poles, that you never know what can come out of that, as if they almost feared me. (Sara)

She also adds a pessimistic reflection with regard to her personal life.

I am convinced that if I had a Jewish mother I would be
married by now. (Sara)

Sara had a Jewish father and converted Orthodox in her early twenties. Danuta also mentions the feeling of not being recognized by other
Jews.

Very many Jews don't consider converts as equals to
Jews born from a [Jewish] mother, that is my experience. (Danuta)

I described Danuta's story in more detail earlier, so let me just bring
to mind her statement about her hypothetical future mother-in-law,
who—as Danuta puts it—"will make her life miserable" because of her
being "a convert." Sara also recalls her conversion as a rather upsetting
experience.

At Beit Din, they told me that I am not a continuation of
my grandparents, and that did not make me happy . . . It
is humiliating and also it reminds you that, at least for
me that's what it reminded me—that you are not a Jew.
(. . .) and of course it's understandable or acceptable that
people look for wives or life partners who will be 10th
generation [Jewish], because I would surely do the same,
you understand? (Sara)

Let me offer a brief analysis of the phenomenon of conversion among
our participants in light of some theories mentioned in the theoretical
framework.

The key characteristic of conversion in our context is the fact that
the participants who converted or consider converting all have Jewish
roots. This has important consequences for their motives. Rambo (1993)
talks about five different types of conversion. The five types are apostasy
(or defection), intensification, affiliation, institutional transition, and
tradition transition. The stories of those of the participants in this study
who have converted in some ways combine these types, although they
do not represent them adequately. Namely, the "Polish Jewish converts"
among our interviewees grew up in a Christian environment (although

not all of them attended mass on Sundays, they all surely celebrated Christmas). Therefore, we could say that they rejected their previous tradition. Perhaps the most relevant type is the one defined as intensification—deepening, formalizing, or revitalizing an existing commitment. Such existing commitment would in our case mean identifying oneself as Jewish and "formalizing" that identity through conversion. The third type is described as affiliation, that is, full involvement with a community one had minimal or no involvement with. In the case of our population, such affiliation also seems to take place. However, the affiliation rarely involves religious involvement. Institutional transition, as the fourth type, consists of choosing one community over another within a major tradition. Although such cases are not present within our sample, in the Polish Jewish context institutional transition could perhaps be applied to (hypothetical) cases of liberal converts deciding to convert Orthodox, or vice versa, and hence switching from one Jewish community to another. Finally, with regard to the fifth category of tradition transition, "Polish Jewish converts" are indeed generally moving from one major tradition (Christianity) to another (Judaism) (Rambo 1993).

The previously mentioned attempt at categorizing the converts in our study according to Rambo's (1993) five types of religious transition is of course merely descriptive and provides a limited interpretation of the phenomenon, as it does not reflect the actual self-narratives of the participants in this study. Let us then turn to another framework for analyzing conversion, which was offered by Rambo and Farhadian (1999). They propose a seven-stage model, which includes context, crisis, quest, encounter, interaction, commitment, and consequences. Let me try to adapt and reapply this model to our particular context of young Jews in Poland as a model, which would reflect the general discourse of becoming Jewishly affiliated both for converts and for those who choose not to convert.

Context in our case should be identified as the environment of post-transition Poland. The crisis stage could be called "discovery"—finding out about one's Jewish roots. Rambo and Farhadian (1999) take the third stage—quest—to be a consequence of crisis, where the individual is triggered to look for new ways in life. Discovery, as we have seen, was not identified with crisis in the accounts of our participants. Quest occurs as a stage of looking for a firmer footing in Jewishness, looking for sites of Jewish content, finding a Jewish community, and finding other

Jews. A successful quest results in an encounter. Again, in our context, the encounter can be understood to mean meeting other Jews or attending Jewish community activities, and it is precisely how most participants described their "first steps." In the subsequent stage, interaction is established, that is, a relationship begins between the individual and the "sites of Jewishness" (again, other Jews and the community center or synagogue), and—as a result—commitment is fostered. Finally, this leads to consequences, which may or may not involve converting. In this way, through a reinterpretation of Rambo and Farhadian's model, we reach a possible stage model of young Poles of Jewish origin becoming involved in Jewish life.

It is important to mention once again the conceptual approach to conversion proposed by Lofland and Skonovd (1981). The different motifs in conversion they discuss are intellectual, mystical, experimental, affectional, revivalist, and coercive. The descriptions of these motifs are generally supported by examples from Christianity, making it difficult to apply them to non-Christian contexts (Bockian et al. 2006). However, even in the Jewish context, they are applicable to stories of conversion understood primarily as processes of religious and cultural transformation (Bockian et al. 2006). As we have seen, the participants in this study do not refer to conversion to Judaism as a religious transformation, nor do they exemplify narratives of different motifs of conversion.

None of the converts among our participants mentions having religious feelings. Their stories of conversion are by no means stories of religious experience. Rather, they are stories of authentication, which in this case consists in upgrading one's status within the community and outside it. As indicated by some interviewees, conversion is a possible strategy to prevent others from questioning their authenticity as Jews. Although this strategy's effectiveness remains under question (the participants often mention that accusations of inauthenticity persist following their conversion), it is by all means the most evident mode of authentication that young Polish Jews can resort to. As we have seen, however, there is a fundamental dilemma involved in the decision to convert. Namely, as a mode of authentication, conversion—in the case of those who do not see themselves embracing religious lifestyle—would entail a sort of betrayal of their own sense of authenticity, or—more bluntly—it would be "fake." The paradox then is that in order to "become authentic" (in the eyes of others), they would have to "be inauthentic" or "act inauthentic" (in their own eyes). For the male representatives of our generation, circumcision becomes an alternative form of self-authentication. However, no alternative rite of passage is available to women.

Circumcision

Beside taking on Jewish-sounding names, another quintessentially de-assimilationist practice in Poland must be mentioned. More and more adult men in their twenties and thirties decide to undergo circumcision. As a surgical procedure, circumcision is very uncommon in Poland, which makes it a distinct "mark of difference." Somewhere between blood and pain, the narratives of those who underwent circumcision reveal a sublime contentment and often a hint of rebelliousness, as if circumcision presented itself as a peculiar act of defiance against assimilation. Indeed, circumcision is assimilation in its reverse, and it is an unprecedented and unique phenomenon in Poland. Significantly, circumcision is more than uncommon in the Second Generation—very few Jewish men born in Poland after the Holocaust were circumcised. It is certainly unexpected if not revolutionary in Polish Jewish history that circumcision made "a comeback" in the past two decades. It is by no means a mass tendency but a very symptomatic one indeed.

On the one hand, circumcision is described with an almost fetishist naughtiness, but on the other, it is seen as a solemn rite of passage in the process of self-identification as a Jew.

> The way I felt about it [circumcision] was that I must really be ready for quite a sacrifice in the form of such an interference in my own body, as a guy, as a person who is generally, not just religiously, opposed to piercings and tattoos, I always thought that marking one's body like this is not my style, that it isn't me, then if I was ready for something as intimate as this, for an unremovable mark like this one, then it is really important to me. And

I felt good about it. (. . .) It has its advantages and let's leave it at that. (Alan)

I am almost 23 and I think it's an age in Poland when many young Polish Jews graduate from college and begin to wonder about their future life, about family, and about their identity, and come to the conclusion that it would be good to complete that identity and get circumcised. (. . .) I definitely appreciate the significance of circumcision as a sort of rite of passage and as joining a broken chain . . . my father was not circumcised, and I think that if I would return to that tradition, I would somehow connect to the generations of my ancestors who were circumcised. (Alex)

Adam also mentions that circumcision presents itself as "one of the most important rites of passage" available to young male Jews in Poland. Only a minority of the participants who have undergone the ancient ritual did it as a religious gesture or as part of the process of conversion to Judaism, where it is one of the requirements. The majority report having it done as a symbolic act of "strengthening" or "completing" their Jewish identities, and they describe it in terms of a compelling individual desire—one that presents itself as one of the most personal, intimate means of self-authentication. In this sense, allow me to note that although it may seem "trendy" or "chic" to be circumcised in today's Poland, having a part of your body cut off in order to make more sense of who you are is by all means beyond "trendy." Circumcision is the epitome of deassimilation. And there is no going back.

To be a Jew in Poland

Earlier in this chapter, I described the ways in which foreign Jews question or challenge the existence of a young generation of Jews in Poland. Some of the presented citations already touch upon the ways in which our participants react to such challenges. Here, I want to provide excerpts from our narratives which account for another mode of self-authentication the interviewees tend to use in reaction to being questioned by the outside Jewish world. Namely, all interviewees stress the significance of the specifically Polish context in the formation of Jewish identity of the post-transition generation. I mentioned earlier that it seems that young Polish Jews are accused of being "strange." In my analysis, I distinguished a category that comprises their individual attempts to explain the uniqueness of the Polish context and thus to "justify their weirdness," if you like.

The first example describes the specific ancestral and cultural situation of young Polish Jews. In other words, it emphasizes the fact that most of them are not "halachic Jews" as well as the fact that they were not raised as Jews.

> It's this specificity of Polish Jewry . . . it is an immanent feature: 90% of the people we have here [in the community of young Polish Jews] are baptized Catholics after First Communion. (Magda)

Szymon talks about his generation in terms of people with "messed up biographies" who are a natural "historical consequence." He says that only the unique Polish Jewish history could yield a generation of people who did not realize that they were Jewish and who now have children who suddenly "want to" be Jewish. Aleksandra also explains that it is a "consequence of history" that "things just turned out this way." The suggestion here is that history determined the character of today's Jewish existence in Poland. It is expressed again in the following two citations.

> If it weren't for the Holocaust I don't suppose my parents would have ever hidden their Jewish origins. (Stella)

> Historical conditions determined the kind of Jews we are. (Ewelina)

In the following quote, Bożena describes the Jewish condition in Poland.

> Being raised to be a Jew is to be told at home that we are
> Jewish, or to be sent to a Jewish summer camp, or to be
> sent to a Jewish school. As you know, there were no such
> options in Poland . . . (Bożena)

Similarly, Max points to certain characteristics of Polish Jews, which
are a natural result of historical circumstances.

> Polish Jews (. . .) are a very specific group . . . (. . .) There
> won't be people among them raised in Jewish religious
> culture, because there were no such people in Poland for
> fifty years . . . (Max)

My interviewees also made statements about Polish Jews being unlike any other Jews.

> I got used to this type of Jews we have in Poland. The
> stories of young Polish Jews are absolutely unique, and
> they couldn't happen anywhere else. And that's what's
> interesting. (Magda)

> Such stories only happen in Poland, one better than the
> other. (Franka)

What seems to be a natural consequence of Polish Jews being
unique and incomparable to any other Jewish group is the fact that
they are difficult if not impossible to understand. Such is the perception among our participants, and it accounts for one of the ways in
which they rationalize why they continue to be challenged with regard
to their authenticity. We can observe some of this insiderism in the
following examples.

> Our problems are often completely obscure for Jews
> from other countries. We have problems that occur only
> here really. Our problems and struggles, that you don't
> know if you should live at a cemetery, or is it a cemetery,
> or is it not . . . for them it's completely abstract. (Eryk)

Along similar lines, Szymon describes the complexities involved in the sole notion of "Polish Jews."

> Before the war there was such a thing as "Polish Jews." Now, you could say . . . that there is a group with its specific characteristics, and you could say that these are Polish Jews, but does anybody from the outside really know who Polish Jews are? (Szymon)

It appears that Szymon is skeptical about the ability of other people or other foreign Jews to grasp the nature of Jewish existence in contemporary Poland.

The two citations that follow use the example of American Jewry in order to contrast it with the Polish Jewish condition.

> If I grew up in the States, I wouldn't have this sort of sensitivity . . . For Jews from abroad, it is kind of weird that we want to be here, that we want to go on . . . (Aleksandra)

> All this [history] makes Jewish life here abnormal, not as simple as it is in the States and maybe that is why so many people decide to live it, because they weren't raised in Judaism, because nobody forced them to run to shul . . . (Elza)

In the next excerpt, Szymon reacts to an often-raised argument which tries to explain the pursuit of Jewish identity among our population in terms of fashion, or a sort of trend.

> People talk about a trend, but I don't particularly like to think about it this way, because I don't think that it's a trend, because most people who do it don't do it because they fancy Jews, but because they have a certain need. (Szymon)

The assumption here, as I believe, is that following a trend is not an authentic act, but following an inner urge or a need already is one. Teresa suggests that what defines Polish Jews is the active pursuit of identity.

> Polish Jews . . . set their [Jewish] identity . . . as one of the
> highest values, and they pursue that identity. (Teresa)

Max talks about Jewish identity as something that cannot be considered fixed.

> It isn't like that, that it's [being Jewish] so super-fixed, it
> is NOT fixed, and that is super for me, that it isn't fixed,
> and that is what is most important for me. (Max)

Once again, we can see the existential approach to Polish Jewish identity as an unfinished and unfixed process—a process of becoming.

Wiktor mentions the fact that young Polish Jews "explore" their Jewishness regardless of whether it is considered "real enough."

> It doesn't matter how or whence someone found out, or
> how many percent . . . mom, dad, grandma, grandpa . . .
> But that someone who is aware that somebody in his
> family was [Jewish], first and foremost has the desire to
> somehow explore it. (Wiktor)

To sum up, authenticity is conceived of as strongly contextualized and conditioned by unusual circumstances. From the words of my interviewees, we learn a lot about those unusual circumstances, but no "essential" definition can be discerned of a young Polish Jew. The interviews in fact indicate that attempts at defining "the essence" of Jewish identity in Poland are futile and that we are dealing with Jewishness, which is complex, unfixed, and "weird." And thus, they seem to justify the type of Jews they are. They talk about the specific Polish context and point to the fact that because of their idiosyncrasies as a group, they are largely misunderstood, particularly by American and Israeli Jews.

One of the impressions we may get from the interviews is that the participants view themselves as members of some kind of elite club. The important message, however, is that they appear to be quite aware of the fact that they act "as if" they belonged to a very exclusive assembly of people. In other words, they are generally self-ironic as they describe themselves as members of a group, which is considered "special."

> I do have this subconscious conviction that Jews are a little bit some kind of elite. (Adam)

The notion of elite also appeared in my interview with Aneta.

> In Poland . . . it means belonging to some kind of elite, being different, I would say it is a certain form of avant-garde . . . the way I see it. (Aneta)

Another interesting category some interviewees refer to is that of subculture.

> I would call the Jews in Wroclaw a subculture. It is a sort of belonging to a group, to a community [but] not religion, not Judaism, not tradition, not a national minority in Poland . . . Simply, [a group of people], who like to fight, argue with one another or love each other. (Stella)

> In Israel, being Jewish is normal and here it is part of some kind of subculture. (Sara)

We can conclude from the previous citations that the "special" character of young Polish Jews as a group is closely associated with the Polish context. The peculiar nature of the participants' collective Jewishness is again accounted for in terms of its Polish "quality" in the following example.

> I think it is like this: Polish Jews are a specific group, the ones in Poland right now. It is a very specific group, whose history caused it to become specific, to become close-knit . . . I suppose all Polish Jews I meet will be much like me. (Max)

We can see here that Max is suggesting that young Polish Jews are bound by common experiences, and those experiences are nothing like those of Jews in other countries. Eryk, on the other hand, mentions a common feature of the group, which presents itself as a form of self-stereotype.

> If I may allow myself to have a theory, then I think it is a question of some kind of abstract thinking . . . the type of sense of humor for example . . . this completely abstract type of sense of humor. (Eryk)

The stereotype of a "Jewish sense of humor" was endorsed by a number of participants, as was the stereotype of the intelligent Jew.

> There are more intelligent people with this specific type of Jewish mind, which I like, the analytic type . . . among Jews than there are among non-Jews. (Sara)

Robert balances between a primordialist and a circumstantialist explanation of young Polish Jews' intelligence.

> Surely, it is partly in that Jews as a nation are more intelligent than other nations, but I think it is a question of selection. The people who come here [to the Polish Union of Jewish Students] come mainly from large cities, and largely from intelligentsia, so that's the main reason . . . (Robert)

Franka explains that what she has in common with other young Polish Jews is "intelligence" and "chic," and she concludes facetiously,

> I don't know if you noticed, but Polish Jews think they are better than others. (Franka)

Joanna, on the other hand, "stumbles over" her own words when she says.

> I wouldn't say that we are better, but . . . kind of. (Joanna)

The final example comes from Max who offers a unique definition of being Jewish.

> To be a Jew is to locate oneself within this whole com-
> plex structure of the European mind, or now the global
> mind, and it is an extraordinary place to be. (Max)

Generally, the participants seem to mix elitism and self-irony in many different ways. Therefore, I present some of the discourse, though aware of the fact that at times it evades proper categorization.

In their honest photographic reportage *Who Will Say Kaddish?* Gary Gelb and Larry Mayer reprint a poignant letter one of them received from a young Polish Jewish woman they met during their time in Poland. Incidentally, she is also one of the participants in this study. The note was her reaction to their journalistic inquiries in Poland, and I would like to recall part of it here as an example of how contested narratives of the representatives of our third generation can intersect with those of American Jews. Her bold letter reads as follows:

> Dear friend,
>
> I can't understand how the same ashes make us—Polish
> Jews—a victim, and you, Americans, a victor. Why are
> you proud to have your photograph at a cemetery? You
> told me you want to put this photo on the back of your
> book. I will never put in "Jidele" [name of a Jewish maga-
> zine she used to run] my picture from the cemetery. You
> decorate your body by light from Jewish ovens. Well, you
> look sweet, don't you? But it's bitter. Yeah, Jewish ashes
> make you someone. Thanks to these corpses everybody
> in the world knows that you Jews are sensitive, and hard
> experienced. The same ashes make us—in your eyes—
> some handicapped monster who—you don't know
> why—has an ambition to be a Jew.

Americans and Israelis indeed play an extremely important role in how young Polish Jews narrate their experience. It so happens that to some extent, foreign Jews were the ones who posed many of the questions which, together with answers or attempts at answers, have become an integral part of the identity narratives of the third generation. Some of those questions were asked directly, others were not. Be that as it may, with the amount of "Jewish tourism" to Poland and the amount of discussion on Polish Jewish subjects, some of the representatives of the younger generations have had more opportunity to interact with Israelis and Americans than with local survivors. Those interactions have been vital in the processes of constructing Jewish identities in contemporary Poland.

PRIMORDIAL IDENTITY NARRATIVE

THE BASIC ASSUMPTION OF primordialism is that individuals are born with certain identity features which determine, albeit only to an extent, their further development. Primordial traits are described as compelling, determinist, involuntary, and inborn. As I mentioned in the introductory section, I am interested in primordialism as a form of discourse. What I want to present now are various types of references made by my interviewees, which I have identified as primordialist. They include statements about identity understood in a particular way, which renders it something we are born with—something that is ascribed, and not chosen, something we cannot reject because it is already set by our personal history, our heritage, our genes, or—more bluntly—our blood. This entails ideas about the nature of belonging to the Jewish people, about the perceived common features of Jews, and about the boundaries of Jewish identity. Furthermore, the primordialist approach is related to notions of perceived essence of Jewishness.

Perceived Essence of Jewishness

The most conspicuous primordialist references in our interviews are those that use the notion of blood. In the following citation, Łukasz associates being Jewish with the idea of Jewish blood.

> Blood. There's something in it, which attracts us. Ancestors. We want to be the descendants of our Jewish ancestors. (Łukasz)

His statement also points to the idea of a primordial bond, which is transmitted through "blood," or genes, which supposedly makes it "natural" for people to feel connected to their ancestors, or to their past. In Łukasz's statement, we can read that there is also a sense of being drawn to the "blood." While blood secures one's connection with his or her ancestors, according to Odelia, it also secures one's bond with other Jews in general.

> Jews always stick together—it is (. . .) in the blood. (Odelia)

Adam makes a very similar statement as he describes the centrality of blood in the experience of Jewishness.

> The Jewish experience is to a great extent about blood ties with other Jews. (Adam)

Danuta describes the very same idea of a bond, which she believes Jews share. However, she does not associate it with the physical attributes of blood but rather—as she calls it—with "something metaphysical."

> . . . That Jewish spark . . . It is something that draws you to other Jews and something that makes you want your life to be bound with Jews and with Jewishness. (Danuta)

In the following example, what is emphasized is the unconscious and—*ipso facto*—involuntary character of Jewishness, as something inherited.

> Some things are simply inherited . . . it doesn't matter whether you know that you're Jewish or not, you will inherit it anyway (Joanna).

To bring up the midrash about Sinai once again, we might say then that it does not matter whether we remember being at Sinai, we will nevertheless always be Jews. The involuntary component of Jewish identity is even more clearly accentuated in Eryk's statement.

> You know . . . it's this kind of blood ties, some kind of
> tribal ties . . . So if you have some [Jewish] ancestor, then
> you're Jewish whether you want it or not. (Eryk)

Robert says blood is "naturally" the most important component
when talking about Jewishness.

> It is my choice that I talk about it [about being Jewish],
> that I don't hide it . . . , but the fact that I'm Jewish is
> not something I had anything to do with . . . I'm Jewish
> because that's how I was born. (Robert)

Robert argues that he "had nothing to do" with his being Jewish. In
other words, he did not choose it. He also says he had a "feeling" that
he was Jewish before he actually knew that he had Jewish ancestors.
Aleksandra also stresses the "roots factor."

> It is the fact that I have [Jewish] roots that makes me
> identify with Jewishness. (Aleksandra)

She also adds that her pursuit of Jewishness is "some sort of ethnic
tribute" to the past. Similarly, Jadwiga suggests that her life was influenced by being Jewish even before she knew she had a Jewish father.

> Even when I didn't have that [Jewish] identity, I mean
> when I didn't know that I was Jewish, we lived as if we
> were influenced by the fact that we were Jewish. It isn't
> something you choose, for me Jewishness is not some-
> thing you choose. (Jadwiga).

She too stresses the fact that she did not choose to be Jewish, as does
Bożena, when she says, "I didn't really choose it, it was chosen for me."
An interesting description of this involuntary aspect in the experience
of being Jewish was offered by Max.

> My experience of Jewishness is the experience of being
> determined by tradition, and very much by my ancestry
> . . . My experience of being a Jew is the experience of not

being able to do otherwise . . . that it determines me,
that it is important to me and that it has to be important
to me, that it is not a simple choice. (Max)

Other quotes on the involuntary nature of Jewishness were mentioned earlier in the participants' narratives of the discovery of Jewish roots.

Jewish Identity Boundaries

The interviews showed that young Polish Jews distinguish between two different categories of converts. The first kind is represented by people who have Jewish roots but do not have a Jewish mother. They decide to convert in order to "secure" or "ascertain" their "status" as Jews. The second category is represented by people who do not have Jewish roots but choose to live an observant Jewish life, and thus pursue conversion to Judaism. The following citations ought to show that although the individuals who fall into the first category are generally considered legitimate members of the community of young Polish Jews, the second category is often frowned upon, and only certain individuals are eventually accepted.

In the first citation, Odelia seems to suggest that the will to be Jewish needs some sort of primordial support, that simply "choosing to be Jewish" is not good enough.

I support people, who have Jewish roots and want to be
Jews, and that's why they convert. But . . . people who
have no connection, no roots . . . I don't know why, what
for . . . ? In my opinion Jewishness is something you
have in your blood, and not something you can attain.
(Odelia)

Similarly, Zofia also admits that she does not understand the phenomenon of conversion to Judaism among people who have no primordial Jewish connection.

> I met people who aren't Jewish and want to convert and
> it's very strange to me, and I don't understand it at all, I
> mean . . . what for? (Zofia)

Patrycja confesses that she is generally more open to people who
are "Jewish by roots" and not "by conversion." Along analogous lines,
Aneta explains that for her there is a clear difference between the two
categories of people ("Jews with roots," and "Jews without roots") and
that there is "something" which those without roots simply lack.

> I don't define Jewishness on the basis of belief in that or
> another God, but on the basis of blood . . . Converts—
> non-Jews—undergo conversion and they are Jews by
> religion, but for me they are not Jews by blood, they just
> don't have that "something." (Aneta)

Similarly, Eryk expresses his doubts with regard to people with no
Jewish roots converting to Judaism.

> Conversion for people with no roots doesn't make any
> sense. It's fake. It's not an ordinary religion, it's con-
> nected with one particular nation. (Eryk)

Note the expression "people with no roots." It is quite natural in the
discourse of the participants to refer to "people with no Jewish roots" as
"people with no roots," and it is particularly widespread in the context
of conversion, as it is used to differentiate between the two types of
converts we mentioned earlier.

Further in the interview, Eryk explains that, in his opinion, conversion is a good way for someone with Jewish roots to strengthen them.
And this does "make sense." Eryk himself underwent circumcision and
admits that he may decide to convert one day (I mentioned Eryk's motives for converting earlier).

Danuta does not say that people without Jewish roots should not
convert to Judaism. However, she asserts that such converts nevertheless will always lack "that something." Zofia also emphasizes this
difference.

In most cases someone with no Jewish roots can never really become Jewish. (Zofia)

The idea seems to be that what a convert needs in order be an authentic convert are (Jewish) "roots." This idea of the superiority of "converts with roots" over "converts without roots" is most bluntly represented in the following citation.

They are not my Jews . . . I wouldn't be unpleasant to such a person . . . but I feel that I am someone different. Perhaps I feel that I am someone better. (Sara)

Again, Sara does not deny "pure converts" (those who do not have Jewish roots) the right to exist as Jews. She nevertheless makes a very clear point, which illustrates the way group boundaries are constructed in our context.

A very interesting remark regarding the attitude to converts came from Adam, whose mother is Jewish.

Converts are considered dangerous not because they are bad but because the people who talk this way don't feel Jewish enough. (Adam)

We can see that the idea here is that some participants possibly feel "threatened" with regard to their Jewishness and therefore they employ discourse which strengthens the boundaries of the community they belong to.

All of the previous citations indicate that there is a strong sense of group boundaries among the participants. They generally disassociate themselves from "Jews by choice," as converts to Judaism are often labeled. In fact, it is the notion of being compelled by a primordial ancestral link which is evoked as the primary reason for our participants' being different from "regular" converts. Let us conclude the primordialist references relating to Jewish identity boundaries with a statement from Sara, who herself converted (but had a Jewish father).

This is the difference between a person who converts and

has Jewish ancestry, and one who doesn't [have Jewish
ancestry]: I really felt that I had to. (Sara)

This reads that for a person to be an authentic Jew according to our
group, one requires the "categorical imperative." In other words, a Jew
is not just someone who *wants to be Jewish* but someone who *has to be
Jewish*. And the self-perception of most of the representatives of the
third post-Holocaust generation of Jews in Poland is that they *have
to be Jewish*, regardless of their baptism and their "unquestionable
Polishness."

ANTISEMITISM

IT IS IMPORTANT TO note that the subject of antisemitism was a rather minor aspect in all of the interviews. More specifically, few interviewees actually made references to antisemitism without my bringing up the question. It seems fair to infer that the phenomenon of Polish antisemitism, although acknowledged by the participants, does not account for a significant component in the construction of their Jewish identities. The general tendency among the participants was to downplay the level of antisemitism, as it is commonly assumed to be very high in Poland. More importantly, though, the interviewees made clear that antisemitism has little direct influence on their lives in Poland. Max, for example, addresses the issue in the following way.

> In Poland, there is no strong antisemitism, one which could pose a serious problem . . . Polish antisemitism lost its teeth to the extent that it can be perceived as folklore, which you don't want to identify with, and which makes you laugh, but at the same time it doesn't threaten you directly. (Max)

Patrycja is perhaps even more blunt as she describes what we could call demonizing contemporary Polish antisemitism.

> If someone wants to create a hell for himself, he will create one anywhere . . . if he sees antisemites here on every corner, and thinks it's impossible to live here . . . then . . . (Patrycja)

The participants appreciate that there is antisemitism in Poland. However, they do not feel particularly threatened by it. Moreover, they have their theories on the nature of Polish antisemitism as in the following two examples.

Polish antisemitism is generally just about ignorance. (Greg)

There is a lot of it, but we certainly won't beat France . . . maybe it's because Poles are weak, and this way they can always blame their weakness on someone . . . And it's not because they want to kill us or hurt us, it's just because they need a scape-goat . . . Most of the time, they are people who don't know what being Jewish is, and they never saw a Jew in their lives, so it's some sort of myth of antisemitism. (Teresa)

Notice the "we" when Teresa talks about Polish antisemitism. When saying "we won't beat France," for a moment she positions herself as a Pole and only later does she switch to "they." Hana also compares Polish antisemitism to French antisemitism.

It's not like French antisemitism with immediate attacks on people, with threats over the phone, with the burning down of synagogues, etc. It's not that strong. (Hana)

The general conviction here is that in the European context, Polish antisemitism can be considered one of the least "bloodthirsty" ones. Clearly, the participants' downplaying of it is also a response to the popular image of Poland and Poles as extremely antisemitic. The participants are likely to defend Poland against such biased opinions, and it seems fair to assume that they do so both as Jews and as Poles.

Alex mentions the idea of "reclaiming" the word "Jew." He refers to the idea that in antisemitic discourse calling somebody a Jew is an insult. Alex calls for the return of "the Jew" in Poland outside antisemitic discourse.

My reaction to the word "Jew" is very positive if someone dares to use that word. (. . .) It's very rare that someone utters the "J" word in a positive context, people are terrified of it, they think it's offensive or too controversial and they try to avoid it in any way they can . . . and so I

heard of "Poles of the Mosaic faith," "Older Brothers in
Faith," "Israelites," and the like. If someone tries to ask
me if I "have Jewish ancestry," I raise my voice and say
"Yes, I am a Jew," because I see it as an act of reclaiming
the "J" word in the Polish language, of owning that word
by Jews and retrieving it from antisemites. (Alex)

As Alex keenly notes, it is a persisting tendency in Poland for people
to feel more at ease with "Jewish" as an adjective and to come up with
numerous combinations of words in order to avoid the single noun. As
a result, we get "Poles of Jewish origin," "Poles of the Mosaic faith," and
other such constructs. Alex's comments reflect a broader tendency on
the part of the third post-Holocaust generation of Jews in Poland to
accentuate the word "Jew" and to give it a new life in their discourse,
where it becomes the opposite of an insult. It is not without significance
that in the language of our participants the word "Jew" becomes a type
of compliment and almost a somewhat peculiar term of endearment.
We might even say that the third generation has developed a type of
internal vocabulary of Jewish words and expressions. Some of them
are based on existing Yiddish and Hebrew words and some are inventions, such as the verb "to Jewify" oneself (*dożydzać się*), which is used
to describe the activity of doing "something Jewish," like attending services, lectures, or Shabbos dinners. Interestingly, one can also "Jewify"
someone else, and this means to encourage a person of Jewish origin to
participate in Jewish activity.

Another word worth mentioning, which has become quite common
in Poland in the Jewish context is philosemitism. The Polish interest in
Jewish things and Polish mass participation in Jewish culture festivals
or other artistic or intellectual venues brought about the concept of a
philosemite as the opposite of an antisemite. For Jews living in today's
Poland, especially in large metropolitan areas, the personal experience
of philosemitism has in many ways become much more common than
that of antisemitism. Controversial as it may be, Polish pro-Jewish activity of the last two decades is complex territory, and a comprehensive
analysis has yet to be done.

INTO THE FUTURE

I CANNOT ASPIRE TO offer here an adequate prognosis of the demographic future of the population of my study. Some of my observations are based on individual examples outside my sample of fifty persons. As an "insider," I am familiar with many more than the fifty I refer to in this book. As inaccurate as such observations may be, when it comes to the statistics of the third generation's choices of a romantic nature, I can nevertheless talk about certain patterns.

Although it can change overnight, and indeed often does, it appears that most of my participants who are or have been within the last several years involved in a romantic relationship are or have been involved with someone of Jewish origin. They are either married, engaged, or involved in long-term relationships with other Polish Jews or "Poles with Jewish roots," and some are involved with Jews from abroad. The vast majority of those who are single are nevertheless interested in dating someone with Jewish roots, and those who wish to have children are generally convinced that they would like to raise their children in full awareness of their Jewishness and perhaps even with a deeper immersion in Jewish tradition. One person is married to someone who converted to Judaism, and together they are raising their child Jewish. The small number of those who are in relationships with non-Jews nevertheless identify as Jews, and most of them continue to be active members of the Jewish community. Conflicting opinions are voiced in Poland by Jewish community members with regard to the general statistics of romantic choices (if there is indeed such a thing) among the third generation. It is a sign of the times that so far very few children have been born who will hopefully one day represent the "fourth generation," and it is too early to judge whether they will secure Jewish continuity in Poland.

Allow me to mention some of the statements the participants have made with regard to their potential life partner and the upbringing of their prospective children.

> If I identify as a Jew, then I don't see the option that my child would not be Jewish . . . Of course . . . it's probable that according to halacha this child wouldn't be Jewish, but at least, I think, if it would be a girl with someone [the potential partner] who has at least some minimal [Jewish] roots, then that would be OK . . . I want to give my children the possibility to be Jewish. If that is what they will choose. (Eryk)

In the interview, Eryk added that he could not be with someone with no Jewish roots. We can see here that he wishes to pass on his Jewish identification to his children, although he believes that it will nevertheless be their choice whether to identify as Jewish or not. Robert made a similar statement.

> My kids will know that I'm Jewish, that they are Jewish, and what they will want to do about it is up to them. (Robert)

Odelia describes more specifically that she would like her children to be raised in awareness of Jewish tradition, although not necessarily as religiously observant.

> I would like them to participate in holidays, to know something about Jewish culture, and about religion, but they don't necessarily have to run about in kippahs [yarmulkes, Jewish skullcaps]. (Odelia)

The notion of "sense of mission" comes back in this context. Having Jewish children is viewed by many as part of the duty to secure the survival of Polish Jews.

> We must make Jewish children! (Adam)

Greg is single, but he describes that he would like to raise a child so that Jewishness would be "fundamental" and Polishness would be "the framework."

Once again, from the interviews as well as from participant observation and personal communication, I can infer that, on the most part, young Jewish adults in Poland would like to marry Jewish. Of course, there are a number of those who declare that they do not actively seek to become emotionally involved with another Jewish person, although they certainly would appreciate it if it nevertheless "happened." There is, however, a significant degree of pessimism accompanying the idea of finding a Jewish partner in Poland. Notably, with regard to the upbringing of their potential children, the participants were practically unanimous in one aspect. Namely, all of the interviewees declared that they would raise their children in awareness of their Jewish ancestry. And in this sense, those children will represent a very different type of Jews.

> I want my children to have it, to not have to ask themselves all the basic questions. I want them to be able to

move on with their identity, whichever direction they may want to go. I just want it to be a given for them. (Teresa)

The generation of children will see things completely differently. For them it [Jewishness] will be totally natural. (Greg)

The existence of the Jewish people is not a self-evident thing. Every Jew who makes a choice about building a family—is the one responsible for the survival of the Jewish people. It is up to him whether Jews will survive in the next generations. Jews can only exist if they multiply between each other. Because it's all very cute—all the little identity problems . . . having a Jewish mommy or a Jewish daddy . . . I mean, you know what . . . it can turn people on . . . interesting little dilemmas and so on, but that is fine in one generation, but in the next generation it's no longer good for the Jews. (Adam)

Again, this sounds like part of the mission to achieve a level of "normalcy" for the Polish Jewish community. And according to our participants, such "normalcy" can be achieved when there will be more Jews in Poland. This appears to be accompanied by a belief that for the next generations Jewish identity will no longer be as complex as it is for this one or that, as Konstanty Gebert once put it, perhaps eventually we will become another "boring Jewish community" (Gebert 2008). It seems fair to say, however, that the children of the representatives of the third generation will not be "ready-made" Jews either, that also for them—as Max put it earlier—their Jewishness will not be "fixed," that it will be a project. They themselves will have to *begin to become Jewish*, and how this process will unfold is yet to be seen.

It is rather remarkable that—as I mentioned earlier—more than half of my participants are in fact currently involved, be it professionally or informally, in Jewish culture, Jewish studies, or Jewish institutional network in general.

Havdalah Ceremony at Limmud, Poland, 2012.

DISCUSSION AND CONCLUSIONS

THE WORLD GONE WRONG

THE WORLD IS ONLY revealed to us when it goes wrong, when it surprises or disappoints us, Arland Ussher observed in 1955. In other words, we discover identity when it is no longer a given but a task (Bauman 2004; Giddens 1991). Such an identity task is necessarily a dynamic and interactive activity, and it happens within a socio-historical and cultural context. For the third generation of Jews living in post-war Poland, the context involves the Shoah, antisemitism, communism, and family secrets—the world gone wrong.

The specific circumstance of the third post-Holocaust generation is that they "stumble over" a possibility of a Jewish identity. They discover that, even if they thought they knew "who they were," they in fact now have "extra material" they can use in the construction of their identities. They can reevaluate their identity construction, as the world is now presenting them with alternative "building blocks." The individuals I talk about in this study are some of those who respond positively and make use of these new "building blocks." My interviewees are people who went on to explore this "potentiality" in them. And according to Bakhtin, an authentic pursuit of such a "potentiality" assumes no fixed sense of self, focusing rather on what is unfinished in a person, on what remains to be said (Bakhtin 1984; Sidorkin 1997). Or—as Milan Kundera says— the focus is not on reality but on existence, on "the realm of human possibilities, everything that man can become, everything he's capable of" (Kundera 1988, 42). In this context, however, it is crucial to appreciate the intrinsic social limitations of human autonomy and freedom (Bekerman and Silverman 1999). At the same time, we must remain alert to narrative as the structure of understanding, whereby individuals give accounts of their experiences, always necessarily in response to a set of circumstances.

> At any given time, in any given place, there will be a set
> of conditions—social, historical, meteorological, physi-

ological—that will insure that a word uttered in that place and at that time will have a meaning different than it would have under other conditions. (Bakhtin 1981, 428)

Bethamie Horowitz (2003) mentions how the term "Jews by choice" became useful in talking about all American Jews (and not just converts to Judaism), when we assume an active assertion of the sole fact of being born Jewish. Applying the term "Jews by choice" to people who were born Jewish can be found outside the American context as well. The concept of "choosing to be Jewish" was mentioned as an idea to promote Judaism among secular Israelis. It has also been noted that in a "liberal democratic society like Sweden all members of a Jewish community are 'Jews by choice'" (Dencik 2003, 99). Diana Pinto (1996a) refers to all contemporary European Jews as "voluntary Jews," who choose to see themselves as Jews and are free to choose their own form of Jewish identity. If, however, we suppose that all contemporary democratic societies endorse the idea of freedom of choice and of self-determination in the formation of identities, what then is the value in explaining particular Jewish identities in terms of choice? To define a person's Jewish identity as a chosen one is largely an arbitrary interpretation. It is in individual narratives that we can identify patterns of identity construction and try to determine how much choice is involved.

A peculiar dialectic of choice and ascription was revealed in my interviews with the representatives of the third post-Holocaust generation of Jews in Poland. As I have shown, despite popular assumptions, the vast majority of the participants in this study describe their Jewish identity in terms other than choice. There exists a set of multiple discourses and circumstances that interactively shape their Jewish experience and how they narrate that experience. The "return of the Jew"—in all of its ambiguity—came unexpected, but its multiple meanings and possibilities continue to unfold through time.

THE DISCREET CHARM OF THE PRIMORDIAL

AS I WROTE IN the introductory section, primordialism and circumstantialism are two types of theoretical positions concerning the nature of ethnic groups. Most literature that tackles with the two theories presents them as tools for researchers to explain ethnicity, ethnic identity, and rules of membership in ethnic groups (Geertz 1963; Gil-White 1999; Isaacs 1975; McKay 1982; Thompson 1989). My approach does not involve primordialism and circumstantialism as theories explaining Jewish affiliation. Rather, I view them as rhetorical perspectives that transpire in individual identity narratives. In other words, the question I pose is not the question of what is the nature (or the "essence") of belonging to the Jewish collective, but what are the ways in which individuals talk about or narrate such belonging. Here is where the dialectic of choice and ascription or of choice and determinism come to play (Melchior 1996).

At first glance, the stories of the participants in this study may create the impression that being Jewish in today's Poland is a matter of choice. After all, we are dealing with people who, for the most part, grew up in Christian or atheist environments, completely unaware of their Jewish ancestry. Furthermore, every one of them could and in fact did "pass for" a Pole and could continue to do so even after the discovery of Jewish "roots." In fact, as I mentioned before, nobody expected of our participants to suddenly pursue a Jewish life and nobody so much as encouraged them to do so. This is why it appears to be the default assumption made by researchers and journalists that the phenomenon we are dealing with in Poland is that of choosing to be Jewish (Pinto 1996a; Rosenson 1996; Winnicka 2003). However, the argument I would like to make is one that is inferred from the narratives of the participants themselves. Instead of offering arbitrary explanations of the phenomena taking place among young adults of Jewish descent in contemporary Poland, I analyzed their stories in search for answers. I analyzed the ways in which they narrate their identities in an attempt to discern the different patterns that surface in the accounts they offer. As I showed in the results section, primordial references were made by the participants in many different contexts. I also showed that the notion of being Jewish as a matter of autonomous individual choice was not commonly endorsed by the interviewees.

Advertising board of a restaurant in Krakow, 2012.

Marius Gudonis (2001a) observed that it has become customary among scholars and journalists to define the new generation of Polish Jews by the element of choice in their identity construction. His small-scale research has led him to conclude that it is in fact unsatisfactory to explain the identity of young Polish Jews solely in terms of choice. In order to reconcile between choice and ascription (the latter stemming from "primordialist beliefs"), Gudonis proposes a distinction between "Jewish consciousness" and "Jewish identity." He suggests that the involuntary primordial elements, which contradict the idea of autonomous choice, ought to be attributed to "Jewish consciousness." He describes the latter as a personal trait which "is not constructed in a deliberate cogitative manner; it arises through a process of social interaction with parents and significant others, particularly during early childhood" (Gudonis 2001a, 135–136). This is where Gudonis's classification becomes troublesome. Perhaps the notion of Jewish consciousness can suit a different population, but in the case of the new generation of Polish Jews—as presented in my study—there are a number of reasons that make the concept impractical: (1) my interviewees could not experience "Jewish consciousness" in early childhood as—for the most part—they had no awareness of their Jewish ancestry in childhood; (2) social interaction—within the Jewish context of their lives—with their parents is scarce, if at all present; (3) social interaction with other potential "significant others"—in our context these would be Jewish friends—became possible and was initiated only after the participants had embarked on the process of embracing Jewish identity. In other words, only those people who already decided to "do something about their Jewish roots" had the opportunity to interact with other Jews.

I agree with Gudonis that while arbitrary assumptions maintain that young Polish Jews are "Jews by choice," concrete interviews with them demonstrate that most of them are far from accepting such an interpretation of their Jewish identities. However, instead of trying to locate these contradictions in "consciousness" or other psychological substance, I highlight the diverse patterns which transpire in the interviewees' own descriptions of being or becoming Jewish. These patterns reveal references not only to essentialist and primordialist discourse but also to constructionist or circumstantialist discourse. Such essentialist/primordialist and constructivist/circumstantialist elements of discourse reflect the two discrepant approaches to identity, which have prevailed in social sciences since the modern times. And the particular accounts of our participants' experiences reflect the ways in which these dominant discourses, as well as social and cultural expectations, condition identity construction at large (Schiffrin 1996).

The Primordial Paradigm

I would like to delineate now a prototypical profile of the essentialist or primordialist approach to identity which surfaced in the interviews. I propose to look at a profile of Odelia, who represents the prevalent attitude to Jewish identity and does not see her Jewishness in terms of choice. She employs primordialist categories in describing Jewish belonging and in addressing the question of authenticity. For this purpose, I summarize Odelia's story, focusing on the essentialist and primordialist remarks, as identified in the analysis.

Odelia was born to a Polish Catholic mother and a Jewish father. She was raised Christian: she was baptized and received her First Communion and the sacrament of Catholic Confirmation when she was still a teenager. She knew her father was Jewish, but her grandmother advised her not to tell anybody about it. She says that even her Jewish grandparents never talked about their background, and because it was a *sensitive subject*, she also never really asked. Odelia only began learning about Jewishness in her twenties. She became a member of the Polish Union of Jewish Students, where she met friends and *entered that environment*. Odelia also started attending the Orthodox synagogue in Warsaw on holidays to *see what it's like*, and she decided to join the congregation officially. She proudly recalls that as soon as the head of the Warsaw congregation saw her looks and heard her Jewish-sounding last name, she was accepted immediately. As far as her parents' reaction to her becoming more Jewishly active, she says her father is simply neutral about it, whereas her non-Jewish mother actually *likes it*. Odelia calls her mother a philosemite.

As far as the young Polish Jewish community goes, Odelia says that there are people in Poland who *still want to continue Jewishness*. The problem she mentions is that it is difficult to establish a Jewish family. Odelia tells me about a relationship she had with a young American Jew who eventually broke up with her, telling her that he could not marry her because she was not Jewish in his eyes.

> A slap in the face—she says—that is how I felt. I feel
> Jewish so what right does he have to judge whether I'm
> Jewish or not?

Odelia goes on to say that she does not want to convert in order to
be accepted as a Jew because "Jewishness is something you have in your
blood, and not something you can attain."

In other words, Jewishness is something you are born with and not
something you can choose. Besides, she is not interested in being religiously observant, and she feels that she should not undergo a "fake"
conversion and continue to live her secular life afterwards. She adds that
if she met a man who would only see her as Jewish after she converted, it
would not be "fair." Odelia says she would only consider converting if she
had children with a Jewish man, so that they would be accepted as Jews.

Odelia supports people who have Jewish roots and want to be Jewish
and thus convert, but people who convert with no connection—no
roots—are people she does not understand, and they "irritate" her a little.
They irritate her because they want to feel more Jewish than her.

> Jews as they used to be, in Poland every Jew had Jewish
> blood, and every Jew has his character, and Jewish char-
> acter is different from that of Poles. Jews have their faults
> and their virtues . . . but a Pole who converts will have
> neither the faults nor the virtues which characterize Jews.

According to Odelia, the most important element of the "Jewish character" is that "Jews stick together." She says that the fact that Jews stick
together is something that is found in blood, and "other nations don't
have it." She also mentions that she can easily identify other Jews just by
looking at them. Even if they are blondes, you can tell. Odelia points at me,
as an example. According to her, although light-haired and fair-skinned, I
too "look Jewish." There are other Jewish features besides looks, such as
certain talents, artistry for example.

> If all those people who convert without roots become
> Jews, Jewishness will be lost. (. . .) I'm against Catholics
> converting to Judaism. (. . .) I feel no connection to them.
> That drop of blood is necessary.

According to Odelia, it doesn't matter whether that "drop of blood" comes from a parent or a grandparent, as long as it is there.

Since Odelia has become a member of the Polish Union of Jewish Students, most of her friends are in fact Jews, or people with Jewish roots, and she feels that this is natural. It is a different type of "sticking together" than the type of interaction she had with her former friends from high school. She and her Jewish friends go through "serious things" together, she reports, and that's the best thing. At the same time, Odelia says that she failed in trying to convince her father to become interested in Jewish things, but if her mother, who is very sympathetic to Jewishness, decided to convert (a hypothetical situation), she would tell her that she had "lost her mind."

Odelia is definitely proud of her Jewish ancestry, and she is involved in Jewish life because of a sense of belonging somewhere. She does not follow Jewish religious commandments, she only likes to keep some traditions (lighting candles here and there, for example), and she only attends synagogue occasionally. However, she strongly favors Orthodox Judaism over any form of liberal Judaism. She perceives Orthodoxy as the most authentic form of Judaism because it is the source: it comes out of history, and for centuries there was only Orthodoxy. This is why, even if there were a Reform, an Orthodox, and a Conservative congregation around, Odelia would "definitely" join the Orthodox one. "Tradition is necessary," she says, and she criticizes the Reform congregation for letting "some goy" lead the service. She also says that she does not mind the fact that women do not have equal rights in the Orthodox synagogue, because it's been part of tradition for generations now.

Odelia says her Jewishness would have come out anyway, whether she would want it to or not. "You have to somehow identify yourself." She has a sentiment for "the whole Ashkenazi culture," for Yiddish, for people from the past, for that Poland from the beginning of the twentieth century, which is why she always cries when she watches the ending of *Fiddler on the Roof*. It is a dream of hers—as she puts it—for Jewishness in Poland to become "something normal."

The Constructivist Paradigm

I chose Iris's story as an example of the less commonly endorsed approach to Jewish identity, where it comes across as constructed and fluid. Iris was baptized and received her First Communion, but maintains that she was raised in a rather atheist atmosphere. She was nineteen years old when she became aware of her Jewish roots. Her grandfather was Jewish, but Iris never had the chance to meet him.

As a member of the Polish Union of Jewish Students, and now ŻOOM—the Jewish Youth Organization in Poland—she started meeting other Jews, and, she says, that is when everything began to change for her. She began attending Shabbat services at the Reform Center in Warsaw, and she says that she now feels "miserable" if she fails to attend. Iris adds that the Reform community does not classify people as "halachic" or not, and everyone is welcome. At the same time, she says that it does not bother her too much that she is not "halachically Jewish." She adds, however, that if she feels it is necessary, she will undergo conversion. Iris maintains that she never encountered a community that gave her so much, where she feels good and safe, and where she can develop her knowledge of things she did not know before. She talks about having something "extra," something beyond regular Polishness. However, she says that she does not want to define that part of her and that she "lets it be" and evolve, instead of naming it, which, she believes, would stop it from evolving. Iris states that she refuses to assume that someone with Jewish roots is automatically Jewish. She thinks it is something one has to work on, that in the case of people who are neither 100% Jewish nor 100% Polish, it is up to choice: they can simply make that choice. Iris goes on to say that young people like herself, who find out that they have some Jewish roots, have the choice—they can either try to fill up that void or give it up.

Iris declares that if she had been born in a regular Jewish family, she would not have had that choice. With everything given, she would not have had the urge to develop in that direction. She mentions having a point of reference and being able to see it as an alternative, which enables her to find herself at a deeper level. She wraps it up with a rhetorical question: "If you're born this way and it determines you, then where is your choice in all of this?"

A Jew—according to Iris—is not someone we can define. "A Jew has to make choices all the time . . . doubts and choices, maybe that's what a Jew is . . . constantly evolving, becoming something, it is never solid substance . . ."

Primordialism is Circumstantial

Table 1. Primordialist and Circumstantialist Discourse

Context	Primordialist/ essentialist discourse	Non-primordialist discourse Circumstantialist/ constructivist discourse
Discovery and Reaction	It was meant to be I always felt different Makes sense	Interesting alternative Cool
Involvement	Inner urge You can't reject it	You can choose to develop it or not
Jewish identity	It is in the blood It is inherited	You can choose to learn about being Jewish
Sense of mission	To be a continuation of your family and of Polish Jews	To spread the knowledge of Jewish life in Poland
Authenticity	Following the inner urge	To have a proper knowledge of things Jewish
Conversion and Jewish identity boundaries	Only people with Jewish roots should convert Jewishness is not something you can attain You cannot just choose to be Jewish	If someone feels Jewish, that's OK You can choose to be Jewish

Table 1 illustrates the different contexts where primordialist and non-primordialist discursive references were made by the participants. Let me briefly review the particular contexts. As I showed in the results section, the "discovery narrative" (the discovery of Jewish roots) was presented by most participants with positive emotion. I have not detected negative feelings accompanying the discovery in any of the interviews. There were a number of participants who describe the experience in a more distanced or nonchalant manner. The most interesting component in many participants' "reaction narratives" was that of a curious predictability of the experience of discovering Jewish ancestry. Many interviewees mention that it was a natural thing, that it was a relief, that it was "fate," or that there was something there just waiting to be discovered. The association with primordialism is evident. It has been argued that primordialist approaches emphasize the irrational, emotional, and imperative character of ethnicity (Verkuyten 2005). Indeed, our interviews show that a strong irrational element is present in the discovery narratives or rather an element of what is commonly perceived as irrational. Similar "irrational" or "emotional" remarks appear in other sections of the results section. When describing how they became involved in Jewish life, the participants describe a "natural" urge to further develop their awareness of Jewish ancestry. They mention the "impossibility of ignoring" one's Jewish roots. In the results devoted to Jewish identity, we saw that two perspectives transpired in the interviews. The first and prevalent one is the perspective, which endorses essentialist and primordialist views. In this approach, the participants express ideas about the inherited and given nature of identity. In the other approach—the constructionist or the circumstantialist one—the participants talk about identity being fluid and multidimensional, "not figured" or chosen.

When describing their "sense of mission," the interviewees referred to two general motives for pursuing a Jewish identity. The first motive or explanation once again evoked primordialist schemes. Here, the interviewees talk about continuity, about feeling compelled to actively be the descendants of their Jewish ancestors. The other motive is, we could say, a "didactic" one, wherein the participants mention the need to spread the knowledge of Jewish existence in Poland. The latter motive, although perhaps "more rational," appears nevertheless closely related to the previous one. It seems fair to infer that the need to show to others that there is a new generation of Jews in Poland stems from the need to actually be a representative of that generation (i.e., to be the historical continuation of Polish Jewry).

As far as the idea of authenticity is considered, common references to what can be defined as an "inner urge" need not necessarily be evidence of primordialist tendencies. However, such references are well integrated in the general primordial discursive profile among our participants. Also with regard to conversion to Judaism, or more specifically with regard to people with no Jewish lineage converting to Judaism, the interviewees were divided along the two general profiles. In this context, the essentialist profile again proved most salient. Most participants expressed cautious and often disapproving opinions about people who want to convert to Judaism despite not having a Jewish "blood link," or *that drop of blood*, as one of my interviewees put it.

It appears that while primordialist/essentialist discourse can be identified in practically every context in our interviews, the circumstantialist/constructionist discourse remains somewhat ambiguous and elusive. The fact is that theoretical expositions of the latter type of discourse on ethnicity mention more extreme aspects of it. Namely, ethnic actors in their circumstantialist or instrumentalist "version" are believed to pursue social, political, or financial interests. In this perspective, ethnicity is viewed as an instrument of manipulation, which is not endowed with any other meaning (Verkuyten 2005). Consequently, we could conclude that individual discourse, which could be identified as circumstantial *par excellence*, is not possible within the framework of an interview or ethnographic research in general. There are contexts, however, where such discourse can be identified. For example, a study of American converts to Judaism showed that three types of converts can be distinguished: the activist, the accommodating, and the ambivalent (Fishman 2006). The study reveals that forty percent of converts to Judaism (the accommodating converts) typically convert for a spouse while having a "warm" attitude to Judaism, and another thirty percent convert solely for family purposes (the ambivalent converts) and often remain reserved or even hostile toward Judaism (Fishman 2006). Of course, we must consider that in the United States the most common motivation for conversion to Judaism is for marital purposes, and hence conversion is commonly recognized as a sociological phenomenon, which does not necessarily entail complete emotional commitment to Judaism.

I want to suggest that primordial identity discourse is commonly endorsed by the third generation because it appears in response to their individual identities being put into question. In other words, the demand for self-authentication calls for the employment of primordial ideas in defense of "identities in question." Since they are new and constantly challenged, such identities could be described as uncertain or insecure. Such insecurity is a function of the perceived frail status of the Polish Jewish community.

Before I further address the phenomenon of uncertain identities in our context, let me summarize the implications of the discursive dialectic of primordialism and circumstantialism in the individual narratives of the participants.

As implied in a number of studies, primordialist and circumstantialist approaches or tendencies need not be mutually exclusive (Gil-White 1999; McKay 1982; Liebkind 1992; Verkuyten 2005). In this study, I apply them as key analytical tools that help decipher the discourse of particular individuals. The analysis shows that even within the scope of a single interview, the two categories are normally not mutually exclusive. Furthermore, the "paradigmatic" profiles I have chosen and described earlier of the "primordialist" and the "constructionist" (I use here constructionist instead of circumstantialist because I see the former as broader and more applicable in this context) "fail" to be perfectly consistent in their "tendencies."

Our "constructionist/circumstantialist prototype," Iris, describes her attitude to people who have no Jewish roots yet choose to convert to Judaism in terms that fit the typical essentialist or primordialist paradigm. The point she makes in this context is that someone who learns about his Jewish roots at the age of twenty years does not actually need to know his Jewish family members in order to know that it is his blood, and he cannot be separated from his ancestry. On the other hand, someone who does not have "Jewish blood" is not determined by "his roots." We can observe that with regard to the boundaries of Jewish identity, Iris no longer sounds like a determined "constructionist." On the other hand, when asked if she would have preferred to be born Jewish on both sides, our prototypical primordialist Odelia—unlike many other participants—answers negatively. She claims that she is perfectly content about having a Jewish father and a non-Jewish mother, which seems to stand in contrast with the very essentialist remarks which prevailed in the interview. Odelia also mentions that her Jewishness is very Polish in that she does not necessarily see herself pursuing a Jewish affiliation outside Poland, if she were to live there. This indicates a particularly contextualized view of Jewish identity, which was otherwise described predominantly in primordialist terms. Once again, all this proves that the way in which people tend to narrate their experience is never fully consistent, predictable, or fixed.

The results considering the coexistence of Polish and Jewish identities brought about another context, which calls for analysis in light of primordialism and circumstantialism. All of the participants were born into Polishness: Polish is the mother tongue for all of them, and Poland is where they grew up. Furthermore, Christianity was the first religion they came into contact with, whether actively or passively. They were educated in Polish schools and familiarized with Polish literature, music, cinema, and theatre. It is evident then that we are dealing with people who are undeniably Polish. Allow me to remark that in public discourse on Polishness, it is the ethnic model that prevails over the civic (Zubrzycki 2001). This is partly because Poland is considered to be one of the most ethnically homogenous countries in the world (Levinson 1998). As we saw in the interviews, the participants in this study all declare being Polish. Nevertheless, none of them declares having "Polish blood." More strikingly yet, none of the participants mentions feeling a special bond with all other Poles. Importantly, the initiation of Jewish identity elements in their lives does not result in a rejection of Polishness. The identity transition of an individual does not involve "getting rid of oneself," nor any mere attempt at doing so (Melosik and Szkudlarek 1998). Melosik and Szkudlarek suggest that it is impossible to "get rid of oneself," or in other words, we cannot erase that which we have been becoming thus far. Generally speaking, the interviewees describe their Polishness in a rather commonsensical way. They see it as a matter of fact. They do not resort to primordialist references in their individual descriptions of being Polish. On the contrary, the interviewees tend to mention context and circumstances rather than irrational or inherent features, which would define them as Poles. The "blood factor" is only resorted to in the Jewish context.

We can observe that Polishness is that part of our interviewees' identities which is not questioned. The participants are not challenged with respect to their being Polish. Their Polish identity is "secure." Their Jewishness, on the other hand, remains in question from within (self-questioning as well as questioning by other members of their group) as well as from without (others challenging their Jewishness). Once again, it is important to note that self-questioning is a product of dialogic interaction with other people, and it takes place within a framework of the prevailing socio-cultural representations and discourses (Billig 1993; Harré and Gillett 1995).

Different categories are used by the participants when they make sense of their Polish and Jewish identities. However, let us further contextualize the two identities as they are narrated by the interviewees. First, in our context, Polishness and Jewishness do not appear to be antagonistic identities—they are not in opposition to one another.

Theories of hybridity provide a conceptual framework, which can prove useful in the attempt to categorize the third generation of Polish Jews. Such theories mention mixing and fusion of meanings, rejecting the notion of homogenous uniform identities (Verkuyten 2005). Perhaps one of the most significant contributions of the notion of hybridity is that it allows for a discussion of so-called "ethnically ambiguous" persons. According to Hall (1988), hybridity is related to the phenomenon of new ethnicities. It also challenges the very notion of belonging to an ethnic group. Moreover, hybridization can be understood in terms of creolization or syncretism, and as such it involves a fusion of old forms, which results in the creation of new ones (Ang 2001; Verkuyten 2005). Hybridity can also be referred to as a "third space," dialogically created to challenge dominant discourses and categorizations (Ang 2001; Bhaba 1990; Verkuyten 2005). Hence, the notion of "hybrid identities" can be applied to "new Polish Jews" in that we can talk about constructing a "third space" between the existing categories of Polishness and Jewishness. Such "critical hybridity" (Ang 2001) with its notion of "third space" necessarily transgresses binary thinking (Verkuyten 2005), allowing for the possibility of strategies of reconciliation and of negotiations between Jewishness and Polishness, although there are no signs of hegemony between the two.

The interviews have shown that Polishness is the context for the participants' Jewish identities. Moreover, the Jewishness they often talk about is the kind of Jewishness that is regarded as an intrinsic part of the Polish cultural landscape. Most of my interviewees call themselves

Polish Jews, and in that sense they see themselves as a specific and, one might say, endangered species, like Siberian tigers, if you like. To ask them whether they are more Polish or more Jewish would be as impractical as to ask Siberian tigers whether they are more Siberian or more tigers. However radical the transition may seem, the discovery narratives of our participants show that their "sudden Jewishness" becomes "naturally" contained in their "established Polishness."

It is important to note that not only the third generation I discuss in this study, but most Jews in today's Poland, are by all means Poles who take their Polishness "for granted" (Krajewski 2005, 101). They "do not need to aspire to being Polish" because they "have been raised Polish" (Krajewski 2005, 17). It is only appropriate here to once again acknowledge assimilation in its reverse movement. Namely, we must appreciate that the phenomena which take place within contemporary Polish Jewish community implore the employment of the discourse of "deassimilation" or "disassimilation," as Pinto calls it (Gudonis 2001b; Krajewski 2005; Pinto 1996a). Being a relatively new concept, deassimilation proves most perceptible in Europe, particularly in Eastern Europe. It represents the individual and communal investments in numerous forms of Jewish affiliation, which are granted open publicity. It is reflected in the processes of embracing partial Jewish ancestries and creating new, public frameworks of Jewish life (Gudonis 2001b; Pinto1996a). Yael Tamir (1996) proposes the term "renewal of identity," understood as a process contrary to the processes of assimilation. She talks about the "renewal of Jewish identity," referring to the process of recapturing a position within the social structure by the Jews of Eastern Europe. Importantly, her term "renewal" reflects a belief in cross-generational continuity, because we are looking at individuals who choose to embrace Jewish identity and in fact embrace an identity that "could have been" theirs (Tamir 1996). They are not returning to an identity which they used to have, but rather they turn to an identity their ancestors once had. In other words, they are not renewing their own identity but rather an identity rooted in their family history, a *potential* identity offered by their past (Tamir 1996).

In the case of the Polish Jewish participants in this study, the time gap Tamir talks about often extends beyond one generation. In most of the cases analyzed here, it was the individual's grandparent(s) who rejected, diminished, or silenced their Jewishness, rendering the parent(s) unaware of their Jewishness or in denial of it. Hence, my interviewees are "renewing" an identity which was already formerly "repressed." Tamir points out that we seem to perceive it to be "less strange" for an individual to adopt an identity embraced by his or her ancestors (Tamir 1996). To be more specific, Tamir asks why is it that we tend to think this way. If, as she suggests, it is no longer expected of a shoemaker's son to be a shoemaker, why then do "we still think it is *natural* for the son or grandson of a Jew to be one too?" (Tamir 1996, 34). Once again, "the discreet charm of the primordial" comes to mind.

In most of the narratives discussed here, the belief that it is "natural" to pursue an identity based on "roots" is a common occurrence. Again we might ask, why, vis-à-vis individuals making identity choices (and changing their lives), do we tend to perceive it as more "normal," "natural," or "logical" when their choices are "supported" by a "link of blood"? A similar question was posed by Gil-White (1999): If most people resort to perceived common biological descent in explaining membership or identity, what then remains of the primordialist/circumstantialist controversy? The question then is also whether it is the case that people are free to choose who they are going to be, but it would be "preferable" if they chose an option which is already "potentially there"? Of course, such "potential elements" in identity construction are unanimously associated with primordial elements. Such is the case also with our representatives of the "unexpected generation": the assumption of the centrality of "blood" is a common one in the interviewees' accounts of identity construction.

If we use Barth's (1969) model for understanding ethnicity and other social identities, which involves the assumption that people may change or adopt new ethnic identities, then the phenomenon of constructing new Jewish identities in contemporary Poland could be explained in terms of situationalism or circumstantialism. Such a view sees identity as situationally contingent and suggests that individuals may, under certain circumstances, change their ethnicity. Our case may certainly appear to embody such a model. However, if we want to move beyond frantic attempts at defining the nature of ethnicity toward an understanding of the experience of ethnicity or identity in general as it reveals itself in narrative, in the stories our participants tell about themselves, then we need to be able to identify the often-contradictory patterns in the ways individuals make sense of their experience. Consequently, we cannot reject the idea of primordialism as unattractive in the study of identity because no matter how socially constructed people's identities may be, or we would like to believe that they are, those same people do in fact resort to a primordial rhetoric. Again, it is imperative to emphasize that primordialism's power (like circumstantialism's power) reveals itself primarily in discourse. We can observe that in communicating or narrating themselves, individuals often resort to primordial terms. We constantly witness people making decisions which very often come across as conscious or rational decisions. Nevertheless, those same people tend to perceive and describe their decisions in terms other than voluntary—in terms of a subjective feeling of being compelled by blood, roots, or fate. The critical point here is that in effect primordialism is circumstantial. In the simplest words, there are circumstances in which people are likely to make discursive claims about primordial factors and to make sense of their identities in primordial terms. Let me emphasize that the idea is not to identify people who are primordial or anti-primordial but rather to identify different approaches to life, bearing in mind that the only way we can access these approaches is through narrative, by interpreting how people talk about their lives and make sense of them.

UNCERTAIN IDENTITIES

ONE OF THE CHIEF conclusions I arrived at through my analysis of the participants' narratives is that the representatives of the third generation of Polish Jews assign more significance to the primordial because they seek something strong, unquestionable, and unshaken to guard their security as Jews. The physicality or the tangibility of blood offers a domain of reference, which seems fixed and inescapable. The primordial type of identity has been described as one "based on features that cannot be changed or questioned" and which "appear to be given by nature" (Tempelman 1999, 17–18). Consequently, it has been pointed out that some groups may use "strategic primordialism" in order to achieve recognition as a cognizable group by others (Tempelman 1999, 25). According to Taylor (1991), one of the important factors in the pursuit of authenticity is recognition—being recognized as authentic by others. Such recognition requires compromise. Tempelman reports that in this sense primordialism can be recognized as a "strategic choice." In other words, for a given group, interference from the outside, which is perceived to be an "existential threat" to the "authentic" identity of the community, may cause a "primordialist backlash" (Tempelman 1999, 30–31). Certain reactions to identity threats, which are discussed by Spears et al. (1997), also appear to reflect primordialist or essentializing tendencies. According to them, in response to threats to one's own group, individuals may (as one of the possible response strategies) display relatively high levels of self-stereotyping, and group members may tend to stress the homogeneity of the in-group (Doosje et al. 1995; Ellemers et al. 2002; Spears et al. 1997). Kosofsky-Sedgwick (1990) analyzed the commonalities between the Jewish discourse of ethnicity and the LGBT&Q discourse of "coming out." She compared gays and Jews in their transition from the private to the public context, and her results suggest that Jewish identification is in fact a more certain one by virtue of it being supported by "roots" (Kosofsky-Sedgwick 1990). Stratton (2000) on the other hand suggests that an abandonment of such essentialism of heredity further problematizes the question of ethnic identification and calls for a discussion of what he describes as "uncertain Jewishness."

The case of Polish Tatars provides an interesting context, which can be evaluated against that of young Polish Jews. Verkuyten (2005) reports on a study done about the small Islamic group in Poland whose members manage an identity of Pole, Tatar, and Muslim. An analysis of their public discourse showed that two different narratives are constructed of their Polishness and of their Tatar-Muslim self-understanding. Namely "in general, the Polish narrative was historical and factual, whereas the narratives about the Tatar past and about Islam had a mythical and symbolic form." In the latter narrative "the prevalent message is nostalgia for the Eastern World, its beauty and mystery" (Verkuyten 2005, 175–176). What the Polish Tatars refer to in their accounts of their Tatar identity is a "metaphysical essence" (Blum 2002; Verkuyten 2005).

The analogies between the narrative constructions among the Tatars and those we can observe among young Polish Jews are certainly noteworthy. First, the conspicuous discrepancies between the narratives of Polishness and their other cultural or ethnic affiliation demonstrate the complexities involved in managing and narrating "hybrid" identities. Second, in both cases, Polishness is described as a "factual" component of their identities or, as I called it earlier, a matter-of-fact identity. With regard to their other ethnic affiliation, both groups resort to ahistorical references or to some mythologized metaphysical essence. The different narratives are presented at "different levels of reality" (Verkuyten 2005). The suggestion with regard to the Polish Tatars is that the reason they construct two different types of narrative is in order to avoid potential contradictions between the two identifications: Polish and Tatar (Verkuyten 2005). In this case, it is open to interpretation whether it is their "Tatarness" or their "Polishness" that constitutes the less "problematic" or "threatened" identity. In our case of young Polish Jews, as we have established, Polishness remains that component of their identity, which they indicate no need to "defend." In other words, it is secure. Jewishness, on the other hand, is existentially threatened.

The critical point is that people are likely to respond to an "existential threat" to the "authentic" identity of their community with a "primordialist backlash" (Tempelman 1999). We could say then that an uncertain or insecure identity is one that is threatened from the outside with regard to its authenticity. In this sense, the notion of authenticity as a philosophical concept becomes less of our concern than the notion of authenticity as a sociological phenomenon. Inasmuch as attempts at overcoming the ambiguity of the term "authenticity" are often futile, in the context of the present study, authenticity proves to be one of the major themes in the experience of narrating oneself. Again, in this context, it presents itself as a sociological phenomenon, which individuals and collectives find themselves responding to.

Note that in contemporary social contexts, authenticity likes to present itself in its negative form: as lack of authenticity, as inauthenticity, or—more directly yet—as an accusation of inauthenticity. This brings us back to Erickson's (1995) remark on the contemporary "climate of inauthenticity" or Cheng's "millennial inauthenticity" (Cheng 2004). We live in an era in which the question of authenticity spreads from Coca-Cola to political hegemonies.

Approximately 267,000 Jews are believed to live in England and Wales, according to the 2001 census. That same census returned as many as 390,000 Jedi Knights of the fictional *Star Wars* film universe. In order to describe certain limitations of the concept of authenticity, let us consider the following hypothetical question: If I choose to be a Jedi Knight, consider myself to be a Jedi Knight, and have some 390,000 fellow Jedi Knights in England and Wales alone to share my Jedi experience with, why then, if at all, should I be bothered if everyone else thinks I am insane, and not a Jedi at all? In other words, does my authenticity as a Jedi require that others perceive me as an authentic Jedi?

This is in fact the key question in most theories of authenticity as well as the basis for the distinction between two types of understandings of authenticity which function in today's social world. At the same time, these two types of authenticity derive from the two general approaches to culture and identity, which I have outlined earlier. The first view of authenticity supports the idea that individuals embody the norms and values of the culture they were "born into," and it therefore suggests that the authentic way is for those individuals to comply with the roles ascribed to them and not to deviate from them by rejecting what was "primordially intended" for them. In this sense, authenticity presents itself as an "instrument of conservatism" (Tamir 1996) and as an essentialist claim. Essentialist authenticity assumes that "a person's real or authentic identity derives from some sort of cultural, ethnic, or biological core element" (Charmé 1998, 3). This is the model of authenticity, which sanctions such notions as "real Jew," "authentic Jew," "authentic Judaism," or some form of "essential Jewishness." We could also say that in this context choosing to be someone who one was not born as, would be considered an act of inauthenticity because it would involve a rejection of the "ascribed heritage."

The alternative to the essentialist model of authenticity is the existentialist model. In the view of this model, culture does not fully determine an individual's course of life, and the authentic life is that which is freely chosen by the individual himself (Stevenson 1974; see also Tamir 1996). Existential authenticity, as described by Charmé (1998, 3), "lies in an awareness and acceptance of our identities' unstable process of becoming." This existential model was proposed by Jean-Paul Sartre (1948) who, as noted by Charmé, appears to have anticipated contemporary non-essentialist approaches to identity in general. An example of such an approach is found in Stuart Hall:

> Far from being grounded in a mere "recovery" of the past, which is waiting to be found, and which, when found, will secure our sense of ourselves into eternity, identities are the names we give to the different ways we are positioned by, and position ourselves within, the narratives of the past. (Hall 1990, 225)

In the existentialist approach to authenticity, self-determining freedom (Taylor 1989) presents itself as one of the central notions, whereas in essentialist authenticity, such freedom is out of the question. In the existentialist model, it is burdened with certain limitations. Two major limitations ought to be mentioned here. The first one is the question of context, which I discussed earlier. Namely, as Tamir (1996) puts it, individuals may be free within a context, but not free of context. In other words, an individual is always situated in a particular social-cultural context which necessarily shapes, to a degree, the choices he or she will make (Tamir 1996). To put it in Heideggerian terms, *being-toward-death* cannot be separated from *being-in-the-world*, from being already situated in a socio-historical context or in a primordial past, which conditions one's existential potentiality (Heidegger 1927; see also Aho 2003). The other source of limitations for self-determining freedom is the premise that a person's identity is necessarily formed in dialogue, and therefore recognition by others is essential in attempting to achieve authenticity (Taylor

1991). Taylor asserts that authenticity requires self-definition in dialogue (Taylor 1989). Ferrara (2004) makes a similar point when he says—following Hegel (1977) and Mead (1934)—that identity grows out of interaction and mutual recognition. Although it is expected that the authenticity of one's identity may not be recognized by some people, it "makes no sense" to imagine that one's identity may never be recognized by anybody else (Ferrara 2004, 20). This is a strong argument, and it clearly illustrates this type of "restraint" to the idea of self-determining freedom in the pursuit of authenticity. And perhaps it also poses a problem for Jedi Knights.

As I already mentioned, it is not the "pursuit of authenticity" as an ethical imperative philosophers still struggle to define, which is of chief interest in the present study. Rather, I try to examine the ways in which individuals narrate their experience and discursively deal with the question of authenticity in a number of its aspects.

In my interviews with the representatives of the third generation of Jews in Poland, a number of patterns emerged in response to the question of authenticity. On a broader scale, the different categories of references to authenticity present themselves as responses to the different types of "threats" to the participants' identities. Let me briefly review the "threats to identity," which can be discerned from the interviewees' narratives.

The first threat involves questioning the legitimacy of the participants' Jewishness. It poses the question of whether the Jewishness of a given individual is a "verifiable" fact. On the one hand, this involves the assumption that a person is Jewish if he or she was born to a Jewish mother. On the other hand, it also involves being able to support one's Jewish origins with some kind of satisfactory evidence. In the case of our population, the significance of the dominant discourse of Orthodox halacha (whose authority remains prevalent in both the Jewish and the non-Jewish world) cannot be overestimated (given that only fourteen of our participants were born to a Jewish mother and have succeeded in proving it).

The main concern that appeared in the individual patterns of self-questioning was the notion of what we could call an "identity without a past." Here, the participants referred to being orphaned and deprived of the Jewish world of the past as well as deprived of a Jewish childhood. The interviews showed that without a personal Jewish past and, consequently, without a personal Jewish memory, certain references appear to the Jewish "meta-memory" or the "meta-narrative" of somewhat idealized pre-war Polish Jewry. Personal memory, which is lacking, seems to be substituted with the narrative of blood as the most self-evident domain of reference.

The main source of threats to identity consists of the challenges posed to the participants from the outside. Also here the results concerning the different types of questioning demonstrate the discursive phenomenon of a "primordialist backlash" (Tempelman 1999). As I mentioned in the results section, on the collective level the different types of challenges mentioned by the interviewees are posed from within as well as from without. In other words, the participants bring up examples of being questioned not only by such outside groups like American or Israeli Jews, but also by non-Jewish Poles. However, they indicate that questions of authenticity are posed to them also by members of their own group.

Without going into detail again about each group in particular, let me mention the most perceptible threats to identity posed to an individual by the different categories of "others." One of the main features in this context is defying the "rational choice argument" of the outside world. In other words, most of the participants repudiate the often-made assumption that they pursue Jewish identity out of individual choice. In defying this argument, the interviewees appear to resort to the "irrational." The participants refer to the imperative nature of the pursuit of Jewish identity (*had to*), to being drawn in that direction, to something inside, or to something metaphysical. Again, the bluntest one is the reference to blood. Moreover, when "accused" of not being "halachically Jewish," recourse to Nazi racial laws appears as one of the responses.

Finally, one of the most prominent contexts for primordial discourse in the case of young Polish Jews is provided by the issue of conversion. Most of the participants disassociate themselves completely from converts to Judaism who have no Jewish roots. This is true even for those participants who themselves converted or entertain the possibility of converting in the future. Again, the reference to Jewish blood is particularly salient here. In short, converts with no Jewish roots represent a phenomenon our interviewees find difficult to understand because according to them Jewishness is something you are born with, and not something you can attain. This view is supported by most, but certainly not all, of the participants.

In Table 2, I review the most common threats to Jewish identity in the participants' experience and arrange them with the respective discursive primordialist or essentialist responses to them.

Table 2. Threats to the Authenticity of Jewish Identity: Primordialist Backlash

Threats to the Authenticity of Jewish Identity	Primordialist or Essentialist Backlash
Proof of Jewish roots The primacy of the matrilinear descent definition ("halachic Jewishness")	Emphasizing the blood link present also in "non-halachic" Jewish roots
Self-questioning Identity without a past	Being the continuation of the past Being the descendants of our ancestors The compelling nature of Jewish blood
Accusations of inauthenticity: *But you are not really Jewish!*	I would be according to Nazi laws Being Jewish is not a choice, it is something you are born with
Accusations of inauthenticity: *Why would you suddenly want to be Jewish, let alone in Poland?!*	Being Jewish in Poland is a duty You cannot ignore being Jewish in a place like Poland
Converts with no Jewish roots as a threat to group boundaries	Jewishness is something you are born with and not something you can attain. Converts with no Jewish background lack "that drop of blood" Only people with Jewish roots should convert

This study cannot aspire to adequately explain the phenomenon of the "unexpected generation" of Polish Jews. However, it seeks to grasp some of its characteristic aspects through an exploration of the participants' own ways of making sense of their experience. Earlier in this chapter, I point out that one of the chief recurring patterns in the participants' accounts of being Jewish is the common reference to notions of a primordial nature. I also mention that recourse to primordial discourse is solicited by diverse "threats" to identity, which come from without, and occasionally from within, the group. Stressing the inherited, inborn, and involuntary features of Jewishness offers one of the ways in which the interviewees justify why they became involved Jews in Poland. However, a thorough analysis of our data provides another perspective in appraising the participants' self-understanding.

Although the interviewees emphasize the significance of being "compelled to be Jewish" by their roots, they also commonly refer to a "sense of mission," where their Jewishness appears to increase in importance because it "takes place" in Poland. In other words, although primordialist references account for one of the ways in which the interviewees make sense of their Jewish experience, "mission" provides an alternative interpretative trajectory. The participants make clear that for them Jewishness is all the more significant because it emerges in the particular Polish context. The notion of "sense of mission" can be appreciated here as another source of interpretation of the existential condition of the third post-Holocaust generation of Polish Jews. At the same time, the interviews show that this "mission discourse" is often accompanied or aided by "primordialist discourse." Also, some representatives of our generation refuse to identify this discourse as one of a "sense of mission," which may perhaps simply indicate a rejection of a certain type of romantic rhetoric.

Although primordial discourse is based on the assumption that being Jewish is "essentially" inherited "through blood," "mission discourse" seems to emerge from the idea that being Jewish is contextually and historically contingent. The notion of mission here can be seen as deriving from an appreciation of the uniquely Polish circumstance of Jewishness. In other words, an emphasis is put on Jewish identity's social and historical situatedness, which necessarily results in its shifting meanings. It could be interpreted as a way for the participants to emphasize their own perceived uniqueness as a group. We could, however, also suggest that this is precisely representative of the idea that in social reality, primordialism is in fact circumstantial. More specifically, perhaps the unique Polish circumstances are in fact the kind of circumstances which solicit primordial discourse. In other words, perhaps what the case of young Polish Jews suggests is that the notion of Jewish blood acquires new meanings in post-Holocaust, post-communist Poland.

Let me juxtapose this with an entirely different context where primordialist discourse was identified. Cohen and Eisen (2002) report on Jewish identity in the United States and mention the phenomenon of "tribalism," which is represented in the belief that Jewishness is a "birthright." Interestingly, the report shows that the "moderately affiliated" American Jews nevertheless stress the fundamentally voluntary character of their Jewish identity. In this sense, they emphasize that they choose Judaism, although they could choose otherwise (Cohen and Eisen 2002). If we compare these insights with the results of our study, we can see that although both American Jews and Polish Jews appreciate the "givenness" of Jewishness as a "birthright," American Jews *prefer* to see themselves as individuals who consciously choose to be Jewish. Furthermore, Cohen and Eisen add that American Jews do not question the authenticity of their choices. On the other hand, the Polish Jewish population of this study generally consciously rejects the notion of choice in their Jewishness. One of the possible ways of accounting for this discrepancy is the fact that, as Cohen and Eisen note, the central arena for the construction of Jewish identity in America is the family (Cohen and Eisen 2002). Family as a unit responsible for organizing Jewish identity is indeed a feature which is almost nonexistent in the contemporary Polish Jewish context. As I have pointed out earlier, our participants are generally the only family members who have an active interest in pursuing a Jewish affiliation. In other words, the main framework for construction of Jewish identity beyond the "self" is the larger communal framework (the local Jewish community or the Polish Jewish Youth Organization). Of course, this has already begun to change, as the older representatives of our population leave their parent' homes and begin to build their new homes and families. To add another observation to this brief comparison of the Polish and the American Jewish contexts, we could resort to an argument our participants themselves have offered, namely that the discrepancies between the two communities are self-evident. Being Jewish in the United States is perceived to be something "normal," whereas it certainly is not in Poland. It may come across as trivial, but it nevertheless is an argument which is emphasized in the interviews, and it is not inconsequential.

Glenn (2002, 140) noted that "throughout all the de-racializing stages of twentieth-century social thought, Jews have continued to invoke blood logic as a way of defining and maintaining group identity . . . It is one of the ironies of modern Jewish history that concepts of tribalism based on blood and race have persisted not only despite but also because of the experience of assimilation." This irony is evident also in the era of de-assimilation in the Polish Jewish milieu. The point must be made, nevertheless, that this "blood logic" takes on different forms in different socio-historical circumstances. For instance, Cohen and Eisen's (2002) report shows that among members of the second-largest Jewish population in the world, that of the United States (the US Jewish community represents approximately 40% of total world Jewish population), being Jewish is considered to be a personal choice, which is not necessarily made in order to ensure Jewish survival (the report mentions that Jewish survival is not in and of itself sacred in the eyes of the respondents; self and family are valued more deeply) (Cohen and Eisen 2002). On the other hand, members of the third generation of post-war Polish Jews prefer to see their Jewishness as an imperative and not as a choice precisely because it is perceived as a call for ensuring Jewish survival. The difference in Poland is that there, everyone is counted toward the minyan, not in the religious sense, of course, but metaphorically—in the sense of being an integral part of the quorum which accounts for Jewish survival. In Poland—as was mentioned in concrete participants' narratives—it is imperative for Jews, half-Jews, quarter-Jews, and eighth-Jews to be saved from oblivion.

To bring up another example of a different Jewish population, a study of Russian Jewry shows that more than half of the Jews of today's Russia would choose to decline their Jewish identification if provided the option (Gitelman et al. 2003). The study also indicates that the majority of Russian Jews associate negative feelings with being Jewish. Importantly, though, there is a growing tendency on the part of the younger Jews to self-identify as Jewish in more positive terms (Gitelman et al. 2003). Also, a 2005 survey of emerging Jewish adults in Britain showed that there is a "strong social identification with the Jewish people" and that they "feel themselves to be members of an ethnocultural group" and actively participate in social and cultural activities, even in the absence of "religious feelings" (Sinclair and Milner 2005, 110–112). A similar conclusion can be drawn from our data. In other words, the type of identification which is most commonly endorsed by our participants can in fact also be labeled as ethnocultural. This label proves problematic, however, as aspects of religion or tradition are rarely completely absent from the identificational narratives of young adult Jews in Poland. Moreover, the declared observant Jews among our sample further challenge this categorization. Be that as it may, as the Jewish organizational network develops and the spectrum of Jewish "options" available to individuals in Poland broadens, we can observe a significant weakening of the religious patterns of affiliation.

AS "REAL" AS THEY COME

ON THE BASIS OF her review of theory and research on Jewish identity in Israel, Hagit Hacohen-Wolf (2005) concludes that the categories and measures traditionally used for the examination and conceptualization of Israeli Jewish identity are no longer sufficient for a proper understanding of the complexity and variability of the process of identification or of the notion of belonging. I believe that this also applies to the discussion of European Jewish identities. The phenomenon of deassimilation, for example, has been noted by scholars, but we still lack the corresponding analytical categories. Krausz's (1993) and Lang's (1993) notions of Jewishness by assent and Jewishness as a matter of choice can perhaps be associated with the idea of an active pursuit of Jewishness characteristic of deassimilation. The two formulations suggest a non-essentialist view of Jewish identity and emphasize identification and an element of choice. They provide a perspective on Jewish identity which is alternative to such notions as Jewishness by descent or Jewishness as a matter of fact (again in Krausz 1993 and Lang 1993, respectively). In these interpretations, Jewish identity is embodied in a stable essence and is determined by "objective" criteria. If we try to apply Krausz's and Lang's juxtapositions to our context of Polish Jewish young adults, we encounter a fundamental contradiction. Namely, inasmuch as on the outside the community represented in our sample "appears to be" a community of individuals who actively choose to identify as Jewish and who often fail to meet the "objective" criteria of belonging to the Jewish collective, when "speaking for themselves," they nevertheless stress the more determinist and essentialist view of Jewishness. This brings us back to the question posed before. Why, despite the proposals of social constructionism and postmodernism, are identities felt and described as if they were essentialist (Bernstein 2005; Benhabib 1999; Calhoun 1994; Epstein 1987)? Similarly, why does a South Korean adoptee in *Blood Is Thicker than Water* (*Blod är tjockare än vatten*) (Trotzig 1996) describe feeling the pressure to define herself as Asian despite having grown up in Sweden?

I would like to mention here the discourse of adoption, which I find curiously relevant to certain aspects of Jewish identity, as described by our participants. Yngvesson and Mahoney (2000) talk about the "subjectively experienced desire for rootedness" which occurs in adoptees who set out to find their birth origins. In Schneider's (1968) classic study of American kinship, we read, "The relationship which is 'real' or 'true' or 'blood' or 'by birth' can never be severed (. . .). It is culturally defined as being an objective fact of nature, of fundamental significance and capable of having profound effects, and its nature cannot be terminated or changed" (Schneider, 1968, 24; see also Modell 1994; Yngvesson and Mahoney 2000). Hence, the "relationship of blood" is what "secures" identity and belonging. Yngvesson and Mahoney (2000) cite an adoptee as saying: "A person who does not know her ancestry is denied access to who she really is." Here again we can see the assumption that the authentic self requires a primordial connection. In this sense, adoptees express difficulties in trying to reconcile who they are (in the sense of who they were raised as by their adoptive parents) and who they "could have been" (had they been raised by their birth parents). For the most part, the participants in this study were raised by their birth parents. However, the late discovery of Jewish roots poses for them the question of who they "could have been" had their ancestors not suppressed their Jewishness in the past. We could say then that by embracing Jewish identity later in young adulthood, they are in fact "becoming" who they "could have been." It is as if they were "really" Jewish by birth but raised in an "adoptive" Polish environment.

In Cheng's (2004) discussion of the complexities involved in adoption, we read, "Does the past or the heritage you didn't know about change the solidity or reality of the life you did actually experience?" (Cheng 2004, 68). The narratives of the young Polish Jewish adults provoke a similar question: Does the new awareness of "alternative roots" pose a moral imperative of some sort to "re-root" oneself? Or is it that the imperative lies within the powerful network of socio-cultural expectations and dominant discourses? "When movements appear to rest on essentialist assumptions, theorists must determine whether that essentialism is strategic, influenced by social, political, and cultural factors, and how activists themselves understand the sources of their identities" (Bernstein 2005, 67). Calhoun (1994, 18) argues that mobilizing essen-

tialized identities is related to the political context and to how particular identity categories have been "repressed, delegitimated or devalued
in dominant discourse." Hence, our context calls for an appreciation
of social discourses' constitutive effect on individual consciousness as
well as of the dialogic nature of human existence (Bakhtin 1986; see
also Bekerman 2001). By the same token, this study emphasizes the
ways in which individuals relate their experience in their own words.
Consequently, it is important to stress that individual narratives are
necessarily constructed in interaction with other narratives. Moreover,
the narratives of the participants in this study show that existing discursive and evaluative frameworks shape the ways in which the individuals
describe their identity transition. However, I find it unsatisfactory to argue that the participants' Jewishness is merely a strategically deployed
identity in the form of collective action aimed at achieving political
interests (Bernstein 2005). The interviews have shown that essentialist discourse accompanied the participants from the very initial stages
of their Jewish experience, when it would be difficult to envision the
potential political interests in the pursuit of Jewishness. Furthermore,
the prevalent patterns of Jewish identification in the interviewees' narratives are of an individualist nature, and there is little indication of collective action on their part. In fact, it is even problematic to categorize
today's Polish Jews as a minority group, whether ethnic, national, or
religious. There is little evidence that Jews in Poland suffer disadvanta-
geous social or political positions, as are attributed to minority groups
(Tajfel 1981). This is most visible in the case of young adults, who often
do not choose to pursue official membership in Jewish organizations
other than the youth organization. Moreover, as full-fledged Polish
citizens, they can choose whether or not to reveal their Jewish roots
to other people. Hence, if falling for essentialisms is part of identity
politics, as a strategy to achieve better identity status (Kimmel 1993),
then in our case we should perhaps move beyond the context of the
Polish nation-state. The better identity status, which may be sought for
by the young Polish Jewish adults, is a fully legitimate status as Jews
within the larger international Jewish collective. However, we have seen
that—as a strategy—essentialism proves to be largely ineffective. Allow
me to mention one more example from an interview, which illustrates
not only essentialism's ineffectiveness but also its potential counter-
effectiveness. Sara's approach to "authentic Jewishness" was brought

up earlier. The following is an extended quotation from that interview.

> Authentic Jewishness is when you're at your window, peeping through the curtain, looking curiously at goyish apartments, wondering what it's really like to be a goy . . .

> I'm not on the opposite side either. I don't wonder what the Jews are doing there. I am neither here, nor there . . . there are two situations like this in Jewish folklore, when characters like that appear. The first one is Dybbuk—a soul, who could go neither here nor there. Not holy enough to go to heaven, and not sinful enough to be damned. One might say then, that I feel like such a cultural Dybbuk. And the other character is in *Fiddler on the Roof*, there is this beautiful scene . . . I know a bird can fall in love with a fish, but where are they going to live? And now, I am such a bird-fish, and where should a bird-fish live? (Sara)

Sara's "self-defeating" discourse becomes apparent when she acknowledges that her own definition of "authentic Jewishness" leaves no room for her. In other words, Sara falls outside her own essentialist categories; she excludes herself from her own definition. Her hybrid "bird-fish" identity incorporates being Jewish, but not in the essentialistically "authentic" way. It also incorporates being a Gentile, although no longer a "complete" one. This example once again undermines the argument that the employment of essentialist discourse is a mere strategy. Sara's statement is representative of the powerful essentialist voice which surfaced in the analysis of the interviews, and whose significance extends beyond its strategic aspirations.

My study reveals that it is misleading to view embracing Jewish identity by young adult Poles in terms of autonomous choice. As I showed earlier, in the participants' narratives of their individual experiences, we find references both to essentialist ideas and to non-essentialist or constructionist notions. Notably, the analysis revealed that the primordialist/essentialist discourse prevailed in the interviewees' accounts of Jewish identity. Essentialist references were common in the descriptions of the experience of introduction to Jewishness and of subsequent

Jewish involvement, as well as in how being Jewish was defined. I also identified essentializing discourse in statements about "sense of mission," understood as a compelling personal responsibility to contribute to the continuity of Jewish existence. We saw that primordial views could be located in most of the significant contexts of the Jewish experience of the participants. The notions of birthright, common ancestry, or Jewish blood appeared in more and less explicit statements. Moreover, an essentialist view of the boundaries of Jewish identity transpired in the participants' approach to converts to Judaism without Jewish roots.

In the personal accounts of the interviewees' experience, the notion of being Polish did not strike us as conflicting with that of being Jewish. We saw, nevertheless, that different categories were used in the individual descriptions of the two. Contrary to the prevalent primordial discourse in the participants' definitions of Jewishness, their descriptions of Polishness can be characterized in terms of context and circumstances. Polish identity is not perceived as something inborn or inherent, nor as something that runs in the blood. Rather, it is described in a matter-of-fact manner, and it comes across as a self-evident and secure identity. Two important analytical implications have been pointed out in this context. The first one is the notion of hybridity (Ang 2001; Bhaba 1990; Hall 1988; Verkuyten 2005), which proves helpful in categorizing the third post-Holocaust generation of Jews in Poland. The second one is deassimilation, which must be appreciated as an unprecedented phenomenon of embracing partial Jewish ancestries in Europe (Gudonis 2001b; Krajewski 2005; Pinto 1996a).

The critical conclusion the analysis yields is that the employment of primordialist rhetoric by the interviewees is facilitated by distinctive "identity circumstances." More specifically, the participants' experience of Jewish identity is accompanied by a wide-ranging dispute on authenticity, and it results in creating possible modes of authentication. The participants' Jewish identities are questioned or challenged with regard to their authenticity and confronted with questions about whether they are "really Jewish" (indeed, sometimes the question is whether they actually exist) and by questions of why they "insist on being Jewish" in Poland. This prompts a "primordialist backlash" (Tempelman 1999). In other words, primordialist rhetoric is applied in response to threats to identity. I have outlined the different types of threats to identity, which incite primordialist references to what is perceived to be unquestionable, stable, given, involuntary, and determinist. The argument follows that the participants find themselves in concrete circumstances which facilitate expressions of a primordialist nature. In other words, let me conclude once again that primordialism is in fact circumstantial.

Because the notion of authenticity proved central in my analysis of the narratives, I described the fundamental distinction between essentialist and existentialist approaches to authenticity as well as the limitations inherent in both approaches. Authenticity deserves our attention in the study of Jewish identity as a peculiar sociological phenomenon. The narratives of the representatives of the third generation of Jews in Poland reveal a wide range of themes which appear to be expressions in response to existing socio-cultural representations and powerful discourses. On the one hand then, the participants make decisions that—at face value—appear to be autonomous choices. On the other hand, however, they enter a discursive environment, where dominant categories transpire and condition the ways in which they make sense of and narrate their experience. By the same token, the discursive patterns we can identify among the participants are indicative of their pursuit of recognition, of their struggle to be recognized as authentic Jews living in contemporary Poland.

Jewish Culture Festival in Krakow 2012

Some years ago, Marek Edelman—one of the leaders of the Warsaw Ghetto uprising—expressed his skepticism with regard to younger Jews "emerging" in Poland in a conversation with Konstanty Gebert—one of the Polish Jewish activists of the Second Generation:

> You guys are a fraud, a literary fiction. The Jewish people is dead, and you have simply thought yourselves up (Gebert 1994, 165).

The idea that "new Polish Jews" "think themselves up" is, arguably, meant as an insult, whereas in fact it can be perceived as a rather keen rendering of the notion of identity construction. And as such, it accurately defines the third post-Holocaust generation of Jews in Poland. The individual narratives presented in this book are precisely examples of how the representatives of the third generation "think themselves up as Jews."

Ruth E. Gruber notices what she calls a third-generation syndrome among the non-Jews involved in the so-called revival of Jewish culture in Europe. It is reflected in "the desire to discover and seize hold of knowledge withheld, denied, or ignored by older generations, be they parents, grandparents, or ruling elites" (Gruber 2002, 9).

It is of great significance that the discoveries of Jewish roots that brought about the unexpected third generation of post-Holocaust Jews are set against the background of the discovery of a new kind of Polish Jewish cultural performativity. The "memory work," which accompanies contemporary representations of the Jewish past is interrelated with the "identity work" performed by individuals seeking a Jewish affiliation in Poland.

The "return of the Jew" is multilayered—there is the return to the Polish landscape (the intellectual and artistic landscape) of "the Jew" in discourse and in imagery, but there is also the "return" of real live Jews. And the "memory work" and "identity work" of both the Jewish and the non-Jewish Poles condition each other in profound ways and have by now become inseparable. In this work, on the Jewish side of the equation, we can notice an expansion of Jewish participation in the often Gentile-dominated field of Jewish cultural performativity, and on the non-Jewish side, a shift can be observed from a nostalgic dream of reviving Poland's Jewish ghosts toward an appreciation of "real" live

Jewish presence. Between the Polish and the Jewish efforts, a somewhat amorphous construct emerged in the form of a new Polish Jewish culture, and with the passing of time we can say with more and more certainty that "the Golem" has come alive. The Jewish mystical legend of the Golem is rooted in the story of Rabbi Yehuda Loew (ca. 1520–1609), known as the Maharal of Prague, who was to create out of clay an anthropomorphic figure and inscribe the Hebrew word *emet* (אמת) on its forehead. This word for truth (or reality) was meant to bring the Golem to life so it could fulfill its mission of protecting the Jewish community from the dangers of the outside world. Jewish folklore mentions different examples of the Golem's unpredictable nature, his insubordinate behavior, and, consequently, the need to remove the first letter—*alef* (א)—from the word *emet* on the Golem's forehead in order to take away his "reality," leaving it *met* (מת)—"dead" in Hebrew.

We must appreciate that the Polish Jewish reality we are dealing with in today's Poland is a product of mutually conditioned interactive construction. And I might add—with all of this metaphor's shortcomings—that this one-of-a-kind "Golem" now has a life of its own, and controlling its unpredictability and monitoring the directions it may go is now the shared responsibility of both the Jewish and the non-Jewish Poles. Amorphous as it may be, it serves both communities, it aids both memory and identity "work," and in this sense it now belongs to both Poles and Jews. And with the delicate line in mind between *emet* (אמת) and *met* (מת), between real (true) and dead, the reality or the authenticity of that reality requires constant care and protection, lest it turn to dust.

The expansion of the social context of cultural phenomena causes a transformation of the factors involved in identity construction. An individual in society becomes endowed with wider access to different choices, leading to the formation of various identifications which go beyond the historical foundations of the construction of particular identities (Castells 1997). In democratic pluralist societies, individuals are free to choose their cultural belonging (Melchior 1993). At the same time, we must emphasize the dialogic nature of identity construction and the significance of social and political circumstances as well as of the distribution of powerful discourses and interactional routines (Bakhtin 1981; Bernstein 2005; Taylor 1989). Aside from such intrinsic limitations to making "free" identity choices, there is the idea that "identity must make some kind of sense" (Appiah 2005, 18). The critical point here is that certain assumptions with regard to what kind of identities "make sense" appear to prevail in the social world. As observed by Yael Tamir (1996), "we think that it is more 'natural' or less strange for individuals to adopt an identity embraced by their parents or grandparents" (Tamir 1996, 34). This suggests that it "makes sense" to embrace a heritage we can claim birthright to. Heritage or a representation of heritage is closely related to a perception of authenticity (see Kirshenblatt-Gimblett 1998). Lowenthal (1998) writes that "heritage like life history must above all be our very own" (Lowenthal 1998, 18). "Heritage is not a testable or even plausible version of our past; it is a *declaration of faith* in that past" (Lowenthal 1998, 7–8). It is in this sense perhaps that young Polish Jewish adults portray their Jewishness in terms of a primordial belonging to the Jewish people, and in terms of what we could read as a "declaration of faith" in the future of the heritage they have a "mission" to continue. "We may be free people," Max told me in his interview, "but maybe we're potentially a little less free than others."

I have tried to show that studies of Jewish identity generate valuable insights not only with regard to the discourse of primordialism and circumstantialism but also with regard to the discourse of authenticity. I would like to suggest that we can arrive at vital inferences through the study of Jewish identity frameworks which are in transition, which are not considered self-evident, which are "uncertain," and which remain in flux. Within the European context, a study of young adult Jews of the Czech Republic and Slovakia could prove especially valuable. Of all European countries, the sociopolitical circumstance of the former Czechoslovakia is most relatable to that of Poland. Furthermore, the post-communist Jewish experience in both countries has a number of shared features. However, there are essential differences that beg for a more comprehensive exploration. Some of these differences are represented by the varied themes in Jewish tourism to the Czech Republic and Poland (for an interesting discussion, see Gruber 2002). There are a number of discrepancies between the two contexts of Jewish identity construction, which we can expect to be reflected in Jewish identity narratives of the representatives of the two communities. It must be appreciated that while the prevailing connotations with Jewish Prague include Franz Kafka and the Old-New Synagogue of the Maharal with his Golem, the associations with Warsaw are those of the Jewish ghetto with its Umschlagplatz. As observed by Kugelmass (1993), "[T]here is something unique about Jewish tourism in Poland. Jewish tourists see nothing quaint about the local culture either Jewish or non-Jewish; their interest is in the dead rather than the living" (Kugelmass 1993, 410; see also Gruber 2002, 143–154). This study shows that existing dominant opinions about Jewish existence in a given context influence people's identity narratives in complex ways. A closer examination of the narratives of the Czech and Slovak Jews could provide remarkable data on the interrelationships, which exist between outside discourses and attitudes and the patterns of narrating identity.

Another contemporary phenomenon, which deserves more attention, is taking place at the other end of Europe, in Spain and Portugal. The analogies between the "revival" of Jewish identities in Poland and the experience of the Portuguese and Spanish "Marranos" have been noted (Krajewski 2005; Muller-Paisner 2002; Pinto 1996a). A comprehensive historical perspective was offered by Melammed (2004). Mainstream debates on Jewish identity could nevertheless benefit from an anthropological study of personal narratives of the representatives of the deassimilating Jewish population of contemporary Portugal and Spain.

Finally, in this study I discuss conversion to Judaism among Poles of Jewish origin. This discussion could be extended to Poles who have no Jewish ancestry yet choose to undergo conversion. Such research would allow for an analysis of the different experiences, motivations, and self-narratives of people with diverse personal backgrounds entering the same communal environment.

This study is concerned with a unique group of Polish Jews, namely, the "Polish Polish Jews," as Stanislaw Krajewski calls them, to distinguish between the descendants of Polish Jews dispersed around the world and those Polish Jews who live in Poland today and identify as Poles and as Jews (Krajewski 2005). I tried to offer an analysis of the processes involved in identity construction as they take place along the ongoing reconstruction of Jewish culture and communal life in post-transition Poland. Inasmuch as the young generation came about somewhat unexpectedly, we can only predict that their Jewish stories will continue to reveal unanticipated patterns of Jewish identity. Moreover, we have yet to see what will happen to our participants' narratives once they give way to another generation of Polish Jews.

As I mentioned before, perhaps some three-quarters of North American Jews trace their roots to Greater Poland. Other foreign Jews also have a special sensitivity to Poland as the site of both what was once the greatest Jewish community on the planet and then the greatest Jewish tragedy in recent history. The destruction of the Polish Jewish community and the overwhelming absence of Jews in that part of Europe have managed to secure an established place in the collective narratives of Israelis and Americans. All this was and continues to be strengthened by "Holocaust tourism." Perhaps not always intentionally, the latter creates an emotional fantasy in which today's Poland is meant to represent a void—a massive "Jewish emptiness," where the foreign Jewish visitor can see himself clearly as "present" and alive. This game of contrasts is there to show the visitor that although Jewish life in Poland ended, it can continue elsewhere, in America or in Israel, and that it is perhaps the visitor's very mission to appreciate Jewish identity, which can survive in him. To appreciate the fact that further generations of Jews are springing up in Poland is to challenge part of that well-endorsed narrative. As a result, for some, live Jews in Poland will always be less "visible" than Jewish ghosts. Jewish presence in Poland is a phenomenon much less familiar to them than Jewish absence. But maybe we could argue that to some extent even the new Polish Jews who discover their Jewish roots are thrown into unfamiliar territory. And in that sense, they are "unfamiliar territory" both to others and to themselves.

Awareness of the dynamic changes in contemporary Polish Jewish life continues to grow, thanks to media coverage, publications, and word of mouth. More and more visitors choose to see not only the sites of destruction but also the sites of Jewish life. Jews become more and more visible in the public sphere. All of this necessarily affects the way Jews in Poland experience and narrate their identities. The perception of Poland voiced by the visitors has always projected onto the way the representatives of the third generation construct their identities. Consequently, our interviews indicate responses to existing discursive domains.

As I have shown, many of our participants mention their own active efforts to explain the Polish specificity of their experience to Americans, Israelis, or other foreign Jews. I find it important to note that over the past two decades such interactions have yielded a few examples of what I like to call the "converted ones." Among them are foreign scholars, journalists, activists, and philanthropists who have become sympathetic to and supportive of the struggle to build new Jewish life in Poland, and who actually believe in the possibility of an authentic Jewish life in Poland after the Holocaust. Among them are such individuals as the Polish-born American philanthropists Sigmund A. Rolat and Tad Taube. Allow me to mention another interesting category of individuals who are not only supportive of the "Polish Jewish project," but in fact moved to Poland. I mentioned Rabbi Michael Schudrich earlier. Among the others are Helise Lieberman and Yale Reisner, who came to Poland together with their daughter Nitzan in 1994. Helise is the founding director of the Lauder Morasha Jewish school in Warsaw, and she continues to be involved in the Jewish educational network in Poland. Yale is the chief Jewish genealogist in Poland involved with the Jewish Historical Institute in Warsaw. They are both professionally and emotionally devoted to building Jewish life in Poland. Jonathan Ornstein, who was mentioned earlier, is the director of the Krakow JCC, and part of his mission is to prove to foreign visitors that being Jewish in today's Poland is a profoundly positive experience and a unique one in all of Europe. Jonathan, who grew up in New York but has also lived in Israel, says that he never felt "more Jewish" than he does in Poland. Ornstein also likes to stress that while it is increasingly difficult to be a Jew in most of Europe, in Poland, it is actually increasingly rewarding and safe. In 2011, Krakow welcomed two more new residents. Social anthropologist Jonathan Webber and his wife Connie Webber, the managing editor of the Littman Library of Jewish Civilization, moved to Krakow from the UK. Prof. Webber took up a position at the Jagiellonian University, where he continues to document Polish-Jewish relations and the cultural heritage of Polish Jews. The Webbers are now active members of Krakow's Jewish Community Center and they both contribute to raising the awareness of contemporary Jewish life in Poland.

Let me mention also Ruth Ellen Gruber—the American-born, Europe-based writer who has long been a keen observer of the phenomena surrounding the "revival" of Jewish culture in post-transition Europe. Ambivalent as some of her conclusions may be when writing about Jewish life in today's Europe, she nevertheless paints an honest and sympathetic picture of some of the most miscomprehended complexities of Jewish culture and Jewish life in Poland.

"We are never more (and sometimes less) than the co-authors of our own narratives" (MacIntyre 1981, 213). And in this sense, perhaps partial authorship of the Jewish identity narratives in Poland should be attributed to those outside voices, whether supportive or critical, that play a significant role in the ongoing process of dialogic interaction. Some of such outside voices are skeptical and provoke self-defensive reactions, which stress the importance of Poland on the map of contemporary Jewish affairs. Other voices, on the other hand, may perhaps romanticize the "Jewish revival." Be that as it may, the representatives of the third generation are just as divided. Some strongly believe in a glorious future of Jewish life in Poland, while others express doubts about Jewish survival in Poland and are likely to express those same doubts at their children's *bat* and *bar mitzvahs*. We must appreciate the coexistence of multiple voices. "Neither the image of a group, imposed by others, nor one produced from within, is capable of representing the complex reality of group identity (. . .). There needs to be a multitude of identities, mutually contradicting but still meaningful if taken together" (Sidorkin 1997, 3).

Can we say that Poland now has a viable Jewish community? Many skeptics still deny the Polish Jewish community the right to see itself as a viable one due to its small numbers. I would argue that new Polish Jewish identities' viability is based less on the number of people than it is on the number of questions Jews in Poland ask themselves and strive to answer every day in an attempt to build a self-awareness of a unique kind—one which is continuously dialogically reconstructed against the outside world.

Being Jewish in Poland is not a matter-of-fact experience. It is intense. Jewish leaders around the world like to use the qualifying notion of a "strong Jewish identity," as if identity was a "thing" or a power of some kind, a fixed feature. But if we agree that identity is a process of becoming rather than of being, that it is never fixed, and that it is dialogic in nature, then the notion of a "strong identity" can be reduced to an idle slogan. The Jewish identity experience in Poland illustrates precisely the very unfinished, fluctuating nature of the process. Jewishness in Poland aims not at an appropriation of its essence; rather, it thrives on not knowing its "essence." It is an identity that hosts questions and contradictions. And its authenticity is that of a conversation rather than a text.

> We have the individual and collective responsibility to
> do everything we can to keep cultural dialogues open

and to allow for the identities of groups and individuals to be polyphonic, that is, to contain a (diverse and heterogeneous) plurality of voices. We have to keep tongues untied. (Medina 2006)

Limmud Keshet Conference in Poland 2012

In this plurality of voices, what the representatives of the third post-Holocaust generation of Jews in Poland say as part of their own narratives must coexist with different narratives construed about their experience by others. For better or for worse, much of what is voiced by the outside world will be internalized by the Polish Jewish community. It is difficult to judge today whether the first accusations of inauthenticity which influence the young generation came from the outside or from within the larger local Jewish community, perhaps from the older generation(s). Be that as it may, when applied in the internal discourse between the members of the small Jewish community, they could turn out to be a powerful destructive force.

Numerous foreign press articles voice bewildered and often patronizing conclusions when trying to identify the "essence" of the contemporary Jewish experience in Poland. Answers are sought for in religious identification, in the Holocaust experience, in "Jewish chic," and so on. Complaints are made about the "tiny amount of Jewish culture that exists in Poland" (Lehrer 2003, 340). If, however, we choose not to view culture as some sort of substance and if we limit ourselves to complaining about "tiny amounts of culture" only when talking about yogurt, we will be able to appreciate that we are dealing with a conceptually challenging dimension of Jewish culture in today's Poland. It is in fact "authentically" Jewish inasmuch as it is inseparable from the real experience of "real" live Jews—those living in Poland today but perhaps also of those living outside Poland but nevertheless exposed to its influence. And if I may suggest a very nonessential "essence" of post-transition Polish Jewish identity, let me identify it as being-in-discussion—in a changing and unfinished configuration of specific situations we find ourselves in and distinct others we interact with and enter relationships with.

A polyphony of voices, as Bakhtin would put it, exists in today's Poland, and it is realized in an endless dialogic play, aiming at no finalization. To be a Jew in Poland today is to participate in a dialogue. "In this dialogue a person participates wholly and throughout his whole life: with his eyes, lips, hands, soul, spirit, with his whole body and deeds. He invests his entire self in discourse, and this discourse enters into the dialogic fabric of human life, into the world symposium" (Bakhtin 1984, 293). Indeed, the Polish Jewish identity narratives hold a prominent place in the "Jewish world symposium." Poland has become a true hotbed of contemporary Jewish identity debate—Polish Jewish issues are discussed in Europe, but perhaps even more so in America and in Israel, where so many descendants of Polish Jews can be found.

This Polish Jewish being-in-discussion or—better yet—becoming-in-discussion takes place in an extremely prolific landscape of content, one that is unique to the times and the land. It constitutes the very organic context for the construction of new Polish Jewish identities. The contemporary "Polish circumstances" are some of the most complex ones in Jewish history and they necessarily affect the construction of perhaps one of the most complex Jewish identities in the modern world.

A "monster" for some and a miracle for others, the third generation is the consequence of all that's happened in Poland over the last

century—the Holocaust, antisemitism, the Nazi and the communist re-
gimes—and all that takes place in the present, including Jewish cultural
festivals, Jewish tourism, and the Polish struggle to come to terms with
its troubling past. They are de facto another chapter in the 1000-year-
old history of Jewish existence in the Polish lands, and as such they will
continue to be subjected to close scrutiny, from the outside world as well
as from within.

Shifting paradigms affect the realm of social discourses, and the relationships exposed in this study are necessarily of a dynamic nature. The
findings of this research contribute to an understanding of some of the
complexities involved in constructing Jewish identities in response to
specific circumstances. The phenomena discussed here remain in flux,
and the individual narratives found in this book are merely pieces of an
unfinished puzzle of identity construction, which account only for some
of the discursive strategies that people interactively develop in order
to make sense of their experience. Perhaps this study can contribute to
the growing understanding of Polish Jewish matters in the twenty-first
century. It may even help shake the persisting conviction of so many
that there are no more Jews in Poland. Finally, perchance the stories of
this "unexpected generation" may inspire some to revisit their assumptions about what it means to be a "real Jew" or—better yet—about what
it means to be in the process of becoming one.

BIBLIOGRAPHY

Aho, K. 2003. Why Heidegger is not an existentialist: Interpreting authenticity and historicity in "Being and Time." *Florida Philosophical Review* 3:5–22.

Anderson, B. 1965. *Imagined communities*. London: Verso.

Ang, I. 2001. *On not speaking Chinese: Living between Asia and the West*. London: Routledge.

Appiah, K. A. 2005. *The ethics of identity*. Princeton, NJ: Princeton University Press.

Ashmore, R. D., K. Deaux, and T. McLaughlin-Volpe. 2004. An organizing framework for collective identity: Articulation and significance of multidimensionality. *Psychological Bulletin* 130:80–114.

Bakhtin, M. 1981. *The dialogic imagination*. Trans. Holquist and C. Emerson. Austin: University of Texas Press.

Bakhtin, M. 1984. *Problems of Dostoevsky's poetics*. Trans and ed. Caryl Emerson. Minneapolis: University of Minnesota Press.

Bakhtin, M. 1986. *Speech Genres and Other Late Essays*. Austin, TX: University of Texas Press.

Barth, F. 1969. Introduction. In *Ethnic groups and boundaries: The social organization of culture difference*, ed. F. Barth, 9–38. Oslo: Scandinavian University Press.

Barthes, R. 1977. *Image, music, text*. New York: Hill and Wang.

Bauman, Z. 2001. Identity in the globalizing world. In *Identity, culture and globalization*, ed. E. Ben-Rafael and Y. Sternberg, 471–82. Leiden: Brill.

Bauman, Z. 2004. *Identity: Conversations with Benedetto Vecchi*. Cambridge, UK: Polity Press.

Baumeister, R. F., and M. Muraven. 1996. Identity as adaptation to social, cultural, and historical context. *Journal of Adolescence* 19:405–16.

Bekerman, Z. 2001. Conctructivist perspectives on language, identity, and culture: Implications for Jewish identity and the education of Jews. *Religious Education* 96:462–73.

Bekerman, Z., and M. Silverman. 1999. Israeli traditionalists and liberals: A social-constructivist perspective. *Israel Studies* 4:90–114.

Benhabib, S. 1999. Civil society and the politics of identity and difference in a global context. In *Diversity and its discontents: Cultural conflict and common ground in contemporary American society*, ed. N. J. Smelser and J. C. Alexander. Princeton, NJ: Princeton University Press.

Ben-Rafael, E. 2002. *Jewish Identities: Fifty Intellectuals Answer Ben-Gurion*. Boston: Brill.

Berger, P. L. 1979. *The heretical imperative.* New York: Anchor.

Bernstein, M. 2005. Identity politics. *Annual Review of Sociology* 31:47–74.

Berry, J. W. 1990. Psychology of acculturation: Understanding individuals moving between cultures. In *Applied cross-cultural psychology*, ed. R. W. Brislin, 232–53. Newbury Park, CA: Sage.

Bhaba, H. 1990. The third space. In *Identity*, ed. J. Rutheford, 207–21. London: Lawrence & Wishart.

Billig, M. 1993. Studying the thinking society: Social representations, rhetoric, and attitudes. In *Empirical approaches to social representations*, ed. G. M. Breakwell and D. V. Canter, 39–62. Oxford, UK: Oxford University Press.

Blum, L. 2002. *"I'm not a racist but . . .": The moral quandary of race.* Ithaca, NY: Cornell University Press.

Boas, F. 1940. *Race, language and culture.* New York: MacMillan.

Bockian, M. J., D. S. Glenwick, and D. P. Bernstein. 2006. The applicability of the stages of change model to Jewish conversion. *International Journal for the Psychology of Religion* 15:35–50.

Bogdan R., and S. J. Taylor. 1975. *Introduction to Qualitative Research Methods. A Phenomenological Approach to the Social Sciences.* New York: John Wiley and Sons.

Brubaker, R., and F. Cooper. 2000. Beyond "identity." *Theory and Society* 29:1–47

Bruner, J. 1990. *Acts of meaning.* Cambridge, MA: Harvard University Press.

Bucholtz, M., and K. Hall. 2005. Identity and interaction: A socio-cultural linguistic approach. *Discourse Studies* 7:585–614.

Burr, V. 1995. *Introduction to social constructionism.* London: Routledge.

Burszta, W. J. 2004. *Różnorodność i tożsamość. Antropologia jako kulturowa refleksyjność.* Poznań: Wydawnictwo Poznańskie.

Buruma, I. 1997. Poland's new Jewish question. *New York Times Magazine.* August 3.

Cala, A., and H. Datner-Spiewak, eds. 1997. *History of Jews in Poland, 1944–1968* [in Polish]. Warsaw: The Jewish Historical Institute.

Calhoun, C. 1994. *Social theory and the politics of identity.* Cambridge, MA: Blackwell.

Calhoun, C. 1995. *Critical social theory: Culture, history, and the challenge of difference.* Oxford, UK: Blackwell.

Carr, D. 1986. *Time, narrative, and history.* Bloomington & Indianapolis, IN: Indiana University Press.

Castells, M. 1997. *The information age: Economy, society and culture. Vol. 2: The power of identity.* Oxford: Blackwell.

Cerulo, K. A. 1997. Identity construction: New issues, new directions. *Annual Review of Sociology* 23:385–409.

Charmaz, K. 1995. Grounded theory. In *Rethinking methods in psychology*, ed. J. A. Smith, R. Harré, and L. V. Langenhove, 27–49. London: Sage.

Charmé, S. Z. 1998. Alterity, authenticity, and Jewish identity. *Shofar* 16:42–62.

Charmé, S. Z. 2000. Varieties of authenticity in contemporary Jewish identity. *Jewish Social Studies* 6:133–55.

Cheng, V. J. 2004. *Inauthentic. The anxiety over culture and identity.* New Brunswick, NJ: Rutgers University Press.

Clifford, J. 1988. *The predicament of culture: Twentieth-century ethnography.* Cambridge, MA: Harvard University Press.

Coffey, A. 1999. *The ethnographic self: Fieldwork and the representation of identity.* Thousand Oaks, CA: Sage Publications.

Coffey, A., and P. Attkinson. 1996. *Making sense of qualitative data: Complementary research strategies.* Thousand Oaks, CA: Sage.

Cohen, S. M., and A. M. Eisen. 2002. *The Jew within: Self, family, and community in America.* Bloomington: Indiana University Press.

Creswell, J. W. 2003. *Research design: Qualitative, quantitative, and mixed methods approaches.* Thousand Oaks, CA: Sage.

Datner, H., and M. Melchior. 1997. Zydzi we wspolczesnej Polsce. In *Acta Universitatis Wratislaviensis No 1940: Mniejszosci narodowe w Polsce*, ed. Z. Kurcz. Wroclaw: University of Wroclaw.

Dauenhauer, B. P. 2005. Taylor and Ricoeur on the self. *Humanities, Social Sciences and Law* 25:211–25.

Davies, N. 1984. *Heart of Europe. A short history of Poland.* Oxford: Oxford University Press.

Davis, F. J. 1991. *Who is Black? One nation's definition.* University Park: Pennsylvania State University Press.

Dencik, L. 2003. Jewishness in postmodernity: The case of Sweden. In *New Jewish identities: Contemporary Europe and beyond*, ed. Z. Gitelman, B. Kosmin, and A. Kovacs, 75–104. Budapest: CEU Press.

Denzin, N. K. 1994. The art and politics of interpretation. In *Handbook of qualitative research*, ed. N. K. Dezdin and Y. S. Lincoln, 500–15. Thousand Oaks, CA: Sage.

Denzin, N. K., and Y. S. Lincoln. 1994. *Handbook of qualitative research.* Thousand Oaks, CA: Sage.

Descartes, R. 1911. Meditations on first philosophy. In *The philosophical works of Descartes (Vol.1)*, ed. E. S. Haldane and G. R. T. Ross. New York: Dover Publications Inc.

Doosje, B., N. Ellemers, and R. Spears. 1995. Perceived intragroup variability as a function of group status and identification. *Journal of Experimental Social Psychology* 31:410–36.

Edelman, G. 1989. *The remembered present: A biological theory of consciousness.* New York: Basic Books.

Ellemers, N., R. Spears, and B. Doosje. 2002. Self and social identity. *Annual Review of Psychology* 53:161–86.

Epstein, A. L. 1978. *Ethos and identity*. London: Tavistock Publications.

Epstein, S. 1987. Gay politics, ethnic identity: The limits of social constructionism. *Socialist Review* 93/94:9–56.

Erickson, R. J. 1995. The importance of authenticity for self and society. *Symbolic Interaction* 18:121–44.

Erikson, E. 1968. *Identity: Youth and crisis*. New York: Norton.

Ferrara, A. 2004. The relation of authenticity to normativity. A response to Larmore and Honneth. *Philosophy & Social Criticism* 30:17–24.

Fishman, S. Barack. 2006. *Choosing Jewish: Conversations about Conversion*. American Jewish Committee (AJC).

Foucault, M. 1973. *The order of things: An archaeology of the human sciences*. New York: Vintage Books.

Franzosi, R. 1998. Narrative analysis—or why (and how) sociologists should be interested in narrative. *Annual Review of Sociology* 24:517–54.

Fraser, N. 1992. The uses and abuses of French discourse theories for feminist politics. In *Revaluing French feminism*, ed. N. Fraser and S. L. Bartky, 177–94. Bloomington, IN: Indiana University Press.

Gebert, K. 1994. Jewish identities in Poland: New, old, and imaginary. In *Jewish identities in the New Europe*, ed. J. Webber, 161–7. London: Littman Library of Jewish Civilization.

Gebert, K. 1998. Don't write us off just yet. In *Dignity and defiance: The confrontation of life and death in the Warsaw Ghetto*. The Simon Wiesenthal Center Online Archives.

Gebert, K. 2008. *Living in the Land of Ashes*. Krakow: Austeria.

Gee, J. P. 1992. *The social mind: Language, ideology and social practice*. New York: Bergin & Garvey.

Geertz, C. 1963. The integrative revolution. In *Old societies and new states*, ed. C. Geertz, 105–57. New York: Free Press.

Gellner, E. 1983. *Nations and nationalism*. Oxford: Blackwell.

Gergen, K. J. 1991. *The saturated self: Dilemmas of identity in contemporary life*. New York: Basic Books.

Gergen, K. J. 1992. Toward postmodern psychology. In *Psychology and postmodernism*, ed. S. Kvale, 17–30. London: Sale.

Gergen, K. J. 1994. *Realities and relationships: Soundings in social construction*. Cambridge, MA: Harvard University Press.

Giddens, A. 1984. *The constitution of society: Outline of the theory of structuration*. Berkeley, CA: University of California Press.

Giddens, A. 1991. *Modernity and Self-Identity: Self and Society in the Late Modern Age*. Cambridge: Polity Press.

Gil-White, F. J. 1999. How thick is blood? The plot thickens . . . : if ethnic actors are primordialists, what remains of the circumstantialist/primordialist controversy? *Ethnic and Racial Studies* 22:789–820.

Gitelman, Z., V. Chervyakov, and V. Shapiro. 2003. National self-identity of Russian Jews. *Jews of Euro-Asia* 2:1–5.

Glaser, B. G. 1978. *Theoretical sensitivity: Advances in the methodology of grounded theory*. Mill Valley, CA: Sociological Press.

Glenn, S. A. 2002. In the blood? Consent, descent, and the ironies of Jewish identity. *Jewish Social Studies* 8:139–52.

Glenn, S. A. 2010. "'Funny, You Don't Look Jewish': Visual Stereotypes and the Making of Modern Jewish Identity," in Glenn and Sokoloff, eds. *Boundaries of Jewish Identity,* 64-90 Seattle: University of Washington Press.

Goffman, E. 1974. *Forms of Talk*. Philadelphia: University of Pennsylvania Press.

Gordon, M. M. 1964. *Assimilation in American life*. New York: Oxford University Press.

Grabski, A., M. Pisarski, and A. Stankowski. 1997. *Studia z dziejów i kultury Żydów w Polsce po 1945*. Warsaw: Trio.

Gross, J. T. 2001. *Neighbors: The destruction of the Jewish community in Jedwabne, Poland*. Princeton, NJ: Princeton University Press.

Gruber, R. E. 2002. *Virtually Jewish. Reinventing Jewish culture in Europe*. Berkeley: University of California Press.

Gruber, R. E. 2009. Beyond virtually Jewish . . . balancing the real, the surreal and real imaginary places. In *Reclaiming memory. Urban regeneration in the historic Jewish quarters of Central European cities*. Krakow: International Cultural Centre.

Gruber, R. E. 2010. Scenes from a Krakow Cafe. *Moment Magazine*. Jan.-Feb. 2010.

Gruber, R. E. 2011. Never better' in Krakow? *JTA*, June 15.

Grünberg, S, director. 2009. *The Peretzniks*. Documentary film.

Gudonis, M. 2001a. Is Jewish identity a matter of choice? The case of young Jews in contemporary Poland. *European Judaism* 34:132–43.

Gudonis, M. 2001b. Constructing Jewish identity in post-communist Poland. Part 1: Deassimilation without depolonization. *East European Jewish Affairs* 31:1–14.

Hacohen-Wolf, H. 2005. *The relationship between ingroup perception and identification with the group: The case of Jewish identity*. Doctoral thesis [in Hebrew]. Bar Ilan University, Ramat Gan, Israel.

Hall, S. 1988. *New ethnicities*. London: Institute of Contemporary Arts.

Hall, S. 1990. Cultural identity and diaspora. In *Identity: Community, culture, difference*, ed. J. Rutherford, 222–37. London: Lawrence and Wishart.

Hall, S. 1992. The West and the rest: Discourse and power. In *Formations of modernity*, ed. S. Hall and B. Gieben, 275–320. Cambridge: Polity.

Hall, S. 1996. Who needs "identity"? In *Questions of cultural identity*, ed. S. Hall, P. D. Gay, 1–18. London: Sage.

Hampson, S. E. 1994. The construction of personality. In *Companion encyclopedia of psychology*, ed. A. M. Colman, 602–21. London: Routledge.

Haraway, D. 1991. *Simians, cyborgs, and women: The reinvention of nature*. New York: Routledge.

Harré, R., and G. Gillett. 1995. *The Discursive Mind*. London: Sage.

Hastings, A. 1997. *The construction of nationhood: Ethnicity, religion and nationalism*. Cambridge, UK: Cambridge University Press.

Heelas, P., S. Lash, and P. Morris, eds. 1996. *Detraditionalization: Critical reflections on authority and identity at a time of uncertainty*. Oxford: Blackwell Publishing Professional.

Hegel, G. W. F. 1977. *Phenomenology of spirit*. Trans. A. V. Miller. Oxford: Oxford University Press.

Heidegger, M. 1927/1962. *Being and time*. Trans. J. Macquarrie and E. Robinson. New York: Harper and Row.

Herder, J. G. 2002. *Philosophical writings*. Trans. M. N. Forster. Cambridge: Cambridge University Press.

Hoffman, C. 1992. *Gray dawn: The Jews of Eastern Europe in the post-communist era*. New York: HarperCollins.

Holland, D., W. J. Lachicotte, D. Skinner, and C. Cain. 2001. *Identity and agency in cultural worlds*. Cambridge, MA: Harvard University Press.

Horenczyk, G., and Z. Bekerman 1999. A social constructivist approach to Jewish identity. In *National and cultural variations in Jewish identity*, ed. S. M. Cohen and G. Horenczyk, 281–97. Albany: SUNY Press.

Horenczyk, G., and U. Ben-Shalom. 2006. Acculturation in Israel. In *The Cambridge handbook of acculturation psychology*, ed. D. L. Sam and J. W. Berry, 294–310. Cambridge UK: Cambridge University Press.

Horowitz, B. 2003. *Connections and journeys: Assessing critical opportunities for enhancing Jewish identity*. New York: UJA-Federation.

Horowitz, D. 1985. *Ethnic groups in conflict*. Berkeley: University of California Press.

Husserl, E. 1970. *The crisis of European sciences and transcendental phenomenology: An introduction to phenomenological philosophy*. Evanston, IL: Northwestern University Press.

Irwin-Zarecka, I. 1990. *Neutralizing memory: The Jew in contemporary Poland* [in Polish]. New Brunswick: Translation Publishers.

Isaacs, H. R. 1975. Basic Group Identity: The Idols of the Tribe. In *Ethnicity; Theory and Experience*, ed. N. Glazer and D. P. Moynihan. Cambridge, MA: Harvard University Press.

Jenkins, R. 1996. *Social identity*. London: Routledge.

Kant, I. 1785/1993. *Grounding for the metaphysics of morals.* 3rd ed. Trans. James W. Ellington. Hackett.

Kelle, U., ed. 1995. *Computer-aided qualitative data analysis: Theory, methods, and practice.* London: Sage.

Kersten, K., and P. Szapiro. 1993. The contexts of the so-called Jewish question in Poland after World War II. In *Studies from Polin: From Shetl to Socialism,* ed. A. Polonsky. London: The Littman Library of Jewish Civilization.

Kimmel, M. S. 1993. Sexual balkanization: Gender and sexuality and the new ethnicities. *Social Research* 60:571–87.

Kirshenblatt-Gimblett, B. 1998. *Destination cultures: Tourism, museums, and heritage.* Berkeley: University of California Press.

Kosofsky-Sedgwick, E. 1990. *Epistemology of the closet.* New York: Harvester Wheatsheaf.

Kotarba, J. A., and A. Fontana, eds. 1984. *The existential self in society.* Chicago: University of Chicago Press.

Krajewski, S. 1997. *Jews, Judaism, Poland* [in Polish]. Warszawa: Vocatio.

Krajewski, S. 2005. *Poland and the Jews: Reflections of a Polish Polish Jew.* Krakow: Austeria.

Krausz, M. 1993. On being Jewish. In *Jewish identity,* ed. D. T. Goldberg and M. Krausz, 264–78. Philadelphia: Temple University Press.

Kugelmass, J, ed. 1993. *Going home: YIVO Annual 21.* New York: YIVO Institute for Jewish Research.

Kundera, M. 1988. *The art of the novel.* Trans. Linda Asher. New York: Grove Press.

Kymlicka, W. 1991. *Liberalism, community and culture.* Oxford: Clarendon Press.

Lamb, C., and M. D. Bryant. 1999. Introduction: Conversion contours of controversy and commitment in a plural world. In *Religious conversion. Contemporary practices and controversies,* ed. C. Lamb and M. D. Bryant, 1–22. London: Cassel.

Lang, B. 1993. The phenomenal-noumenal Jew. In *Jewish identity,* ed. D. T Goldberg and M. Krausz, 279–90. Philadelphia: Temple University Press.

Lehrer, E. 2003. Repopulating Jewish Poland—in wood. *Polin: Studies in Polish Jewry* 16:335–55.

Levinson, D. 1998. *Ethnic groups worldwide.* Phoenix, AR: Oryx.

Levi-Strauss, C. 1963–1976. *Structural anthropology.* New York: Basic Books.

Liebkind, K. 1992. Ethnic identity—challenging the boundaries of social psychology. In *Social psychology of identity and the self-concept,* ed. G. M. Breakwell, 147–85. London: Surrey University Press.

Lieblich, A., R. Tuval-Mashiach, and T. Zilber. 1998. *Narrative research: Reading, analysis, and interpretation.* Thousand Oaks, CA: Sage Publications.

Lifton, R. J. 1993. *The Protean self: Human resilience in an age of fragmentation.* New York: Basic Books.

Locke, J. 1997. *An essay concerning human understanding.* Ed. R. Woolhouse. London: Penguin Books.

Lofland, J., and N. Skonovd. 1981. Conversion motifs. *Journal for the Scientific Study of Religion* 20:373–85.

Lowenthal, D. 1998. Fabricating heritage. *History and Memory* 10:5–24.

MacIntyre, A. 1981. *After virtue*. Notre Dame, IN: University of Notre Dame Press.

Makuch, J. 2009. The Jewish Culture Festival: Between two worlds. In *Reclaiming memory. Urban regeneration in the historic Jewish quarters of Central European cities*. Krakow: International Cultural Centre.

Marcus, G. E., and M. Fischer. 1986. *Anthropology as cultural critique: An experimental moment in the human sciences*. Chicago: University of Chicago Press.

Margalit, A., and J. Raz. 1990. National self-determination. *Journal of Philosophy* 87:439–61.

Mariner, R. 1999. Conversion to Judaism: A tale of the good, the bad and the ungrateful. In *Religious conversion: Contemporary practices and controversies*, ed. C. Lamb and M. D. Bryant, 89–101. London: Cassell.

Mason, J. 1996. *Qualitative researching*. London: Sage.

Mayer, L. N., and G. Gelb. 2002. *Who will say kaddish?: A search for Jewish identity in contemporary Poland*. Syracuse, NY: Syracuse University Press.

Maykut, P., and R. Morehouse. 1994. *Beginning qualitative research: A philosophic and practical guide*. London: The Falmer Press.

McAdams, D. P., R. Josselson, A. Lieblich. 2001. *Turns in the road: Narrative studies of lives in transition*. Washington DC: American Psychological Association.

McKay, J. 1982. An exploratory synthesis of primordial and mobilizationist approaches to ethnic phenomena. *Ethnic and Racial Studies* 5:395–420.

Mead, G. H. 1934. *Mind, self, and society*. Chicago: University of Chicago.

Mead, M. 1964. *Continuities in cultural evolution*. New Haven: Yale University Press.

Medina, J. 2006. Tongues untied: Polyphonic identities and the Hispanic family. *Ethnic Studies Review* 29(1): 1-21.

Melammed, R. L. 2004. *A question of identity: Iberian Conversos in historical perspective*. Oxford: Oxford University Press.

Melchior, M. 1990. *Social identity of an individual* [in Polish]. Warsaw: University of Warsaw Institute of Applied Social Studies.

Melchior, M. 1993. Kategoria tożsamości jako wyzwanie badawcze. In *Kulturowy wymiar przemian spolecznych*, ed. A. Jawlowska, M. Kempny, and E. Tarkowska, 235–47. Warsaw: IFiS PAN.

Melchior, M. 1996. Jewish Identity in Poland: Between Ascription and Choice. In *A Quest for Identity. Post War Jewish Biographies,* ed. Y. Kashti, F. Eros, D. Schers, D. Zisenwine, 95-110, Studies in Jewish Culture Identity and Community. School of Education - Tel Aviv University, Israel [in English].

Melosik, Z., and T. Szkudlarek. 1998. *Kultura, tozsamosc i edukacja. Migotanie znaczen*. Krakow: Impuls.

Michlic, J. 2006. *Poland's Threatening Other: The Image of the Jew from 1880 to the Present. Lincoln: University of Nebraska Press.*

Mill, J. S. 1869. *On Liberty*. London: Longman, Roberts & Green.

Mill, J. S. 1884. *A system of logic*. London: Longman, Roberts & Green.

Modell, J. S. 1994. *Kinship with strangers: Adoption and interpretations of kinship in American Culture*. Berkeley: University of California Press.

Muller-Paisner, V. 2002. Poland: Crises in Christian-Jewish identity. *Journal of Applied Psychoanalytic Studies* 4:13–30.

Nagel, J. 1994. Constructing ethnicity: Creating and recreating ethnic identity and culture. *Social Problems* 41:52–76.

Nairn, R., and T. N. McCreanor. 1991. Race talk and common sense: Patterns of discourse on Maori/Pakeha relations in New Zealand. *Journal of Language and Social Psychology* 10:245–62.

Niezabitowska, M., and T. Tomaszewski. 1986. Remnants—The last Jews of Poland. *National Geographic*. September.

Ochs, E., and L. Capps. 1996. Narrating the self. *Annual Review of Anthropology* 25:19–43.

Orla-Bukowska, A., and R. D. Cherry. 2007. *Rethinking Poles and Jews: Troubled past, brighter future*. New York: Rowman & Littlefield.

Phinney, J. 2003. Ethnic identity and acculturation. In *Acculturation: Advances in theory, measurement, and applied research*, ed. K. Chun, P. B. Organista, and G. Martin, 63–81. Washington DC: American Psychological Association.

Piccone, P. 1992–1993. The actuality of traditions. *Telos* 94:89–102.

Pinto, D. 1996a. *A new Jewish identity for post-1989 Europe*. Policy Paper 1. Jewish Policy Research, London.

Pinto, D. 1996b. Fifty years after the Holocaust: Building a new Jewish and Polish memory. *Eastern European Jewish Affairs* 26:79–95.

Polonsky, A., I. Bartal, G. Hundert, M. Opalski, and J. Tomaszewski, eds. 1996. *Jews, Poles, Socialists: The failure of an ideal*. Vol. 9. London: The Littman Library of Jewish Civilization.

Potter, J., and M. Wetherell. 1987. *Discourse and social psychology: Beyond attitudes and behaviour*. London: Sage.

Pragier, R. 1992. *Żydzi czy Polacy?* Warsaw: Rytm.

Propp, V. 1968. *Morphology of the folktale*. Austin: University of Texas Press.

Punch, K. F. 1998. *Introduction to social research: Quantitative and qualitative approaches*. London: Sage.

Rambo, L. R., and C. E. Farhadian. 1999. Converting: Stages of religious change. In *Religious conversion: Contemporary practices and controversies*, ed. C. Lamb and

M. D. Bryant, 23–34. London: Cassell.

Rambo, L. R. 1993. *Understanding religious conversion*. New Haven: Yale University Press.

Redlich, S. 2011. *Life in transit: Jews in post-war Lodz, 1945–1950*. Boston: Academic Studies Press.

Riessman, C. J. 1993. *Narrative analysis*. Newbury Park, CA: Sage.

Rosenson, C.A. 1996. Jewish identity construction in contemporary Poland: Dialogue between generations. *East European Jewish Affairs* 26:67–79.

Rosenson, C.A. 2003. Polish Jewish institutions in transition: Personalities over process. In *New Jewish identities: Contemporary Europe and beyond*, ed. Z. Gitelman, B. Kosmin, and A. Kovacs, 263–90. Budapest: CEU Press.

Rosenwald, G. C., and R. L. Ochberg. 1992. Introduction: Life stories, cultural politics, and self-understanding. In *Storied lives. The cultural politics of self-understanding*, ed. G. C. Rosenwald and R. L. Ochberg, 1–18. New Haven: Yale University Press.

Rosner, K. 2003. *Narracja, tożsamość i czas*. Krakow: Universitas.

Rousseau, J. J. 1973/2000. *Confessions*. Trans. A Scholar. Oxford: Oxford University Press.

Sagi, A. 2002. *A critique of Jewish identity discourse*. Ramat Gan: Bar Ilan University.

Sagi, A., and Z. Zohar. 1994. *Conversion to Judaism and the meaning of Jewish identity* [in Hebrew]. Jerusalem: The Bialik Institute.

Sartre, J-P. 1948. *Anti-Semite and Jew*. New York: Schocken.

Schachter, E. P. 2005a. Erikson meets the postmodern: Can classic identity theory rise to the challenge? *An International Journal of Theory and Research* 5:137–60.

Schachter, E. P. 2005b. Context and identity formation: A theoretical analysis and a case study. *Journal of Adolescent Research* 20:375–95.

Schatz, J. 1991. *The generation: The rise and fall of the Jewish communists in Poland*. Berkeley: University of California Press.

Schiffrin, D. 1996. Narrative as self-portrait: Sociolinguistic constructions of identity. *Language in society* 25:167–203.

Schischa, R., and D. Berenstein. 2002. *Mapping Jewish culture in Europe today: A pilot project*. Policy Paper 3. Jewish Policy Research, London.

Schneider, D. M. 1968. *American kinship: A cultural account*. Chicago, IL: University of Chicago Press.

Selzer, M. 1968. Who are the Jews? A guide for the perplexed Gentile—and Jew. *Phylon (1960–)* 29:231–44.

Shils, E. 1957. Primordial, personal, sacred and civil ties. *British Journal of Sociology* 8:130–45.

Shkedi, A., and G. Horenczyk. 1995. The role of teacher ideology in the teaching of culturally valued texts. *Teaching and Teacher Education* 11:107–17.

Sidorkin, A. M. 1997. *Authenticity—dialogicality—recognition: An improbable journey*.

Faculty Publications. Paper 22. http://digitalcommons.ric.edu/faculty public-
ations/22

Simon, B. 2004. *Identity in modern society. A social psychological perspective.* Oxford:
Blackwell.

Sinclair, J., and D. Milner. 2005. On being Jewish: A qualitative study of identity
among British Jews in emerging adulthood. *Journal of Adolescent Research*
20:91–117.

Smith, A. D. 1987. *The ethnic origins of nations.* New York: B. Blackwell.

Smith, A. D. 1992. The question of Jewish identity. In *A new Jewry? America since
the Second World War*, ed. P. Y Medding, New York: Oxford University Press.

Smith, A. D. 1998. *Nationalism and Modernism.* London: Routledge.

Smith, A. D. 2001. *Nationalism.* Cambridge: Polity Press.

Spears, R., B. Doosje, and N. Ellemers. 1997. Self-stereotyping in the face of threats
to group status and distinctiveness: The role of group identification. *Personality
and Social Psychology Bulletin* 23:538–53.

Spradley, J. P. 1979. *The ethnographic interview.* New York: Holt, Rinehart &
Winston.

Stevenson, L. 1974. *Seven theories of human nature.* Oxford: Oxford University
Press.

Stratton, J. 2000. *Coming out Jewish: Constructing ambivalent identities.* London:
Routledge.

Strauss, A., and J. Corbin. 1994. Grounded theory methodology: An overview. In
Handbook of qualitative research, ed. N. K. Dezdin and Y. S. Lincoln, 273–85.
Thousand Oaks, CA: Sage.

Sułek, A. 1999. Ilu jest Żydów w Polsce? Ekperymentalne studium wpływu skali
na odpowiedzi ankietowe. In *Spojrzenie na metode. Studia z metodologii badan
socjologicznych*, ed. K. L. H. Domanski and A. Rostocki, Warsaw: IFiS PAN
96-104.

Surdykowski, J. 2005. Historia Panny S. In *Newsweek Polska* 35/2005, 68-71.

Świda-Ziemba, H. 2005. *Młodzi w nowym świecie.* Kraków: Wydawnictwo Literackie.

Tajfel, H. 1981. *Human groups and social categories.* Cambridge: Cambridge
University Press.

Tamir, Y. 1996. Some thoughts regarding the phrase: "A quest for identity." In *A
quest for identity: Post war biographies*, ed. F. E. Y. Kashti, D. Schers, and D.
Zisenwine, 21–50. Tel Aviv: Tel Aviv University.

Taylor, C. 1989. *Sources of the self: The making of modern identity.* Cambridge:
Cambridge University Press.

Taylor, C. 1991. *The ethics of authenticity.* Cambridge, MA: Harvard University Press.

Tempelman, S. 1999. Constructions of cultural identity: Multiculturalism and ex-
clusion. *Political Studies* 47:17–31.

Thompson, R. 1989. *Theories of ethnicity. A critical appraisal.* Westport, CT:
Greenwood Press.

Tomashevski, B. 1965. Thematics. In *Russian formalist criticism: Four essays*, ed. L. Lemon and M. Reis. Lincoln: University Nebraska Press.

Tomasi, J. 1995. Kymlicka, liberalism, and respect for cultural minorities. *Ethics* 105:580–603.

Toolan, M. 1988. *Narrative: A critical linguistic introduction*. London: Routledge.

Trotzig, A. 1996. *Blod är tjockare än vatten [Blood is thicker than water]*. Stockholm: Bonniers Verlag.

Ury, S. 2000. Who, what, when, where, and why is Polish Jewry? Envisioning, constructing, and possessing Polish Jewry. *Jewish Social Studies* 6:205–29.

Ussher, A. 1955. *Journey through dread*. New York: The Delvin Aldar Company.

Verkuyten, M. 2005. *The social psychology of ethnic identity*. Hove: Psychology Press.

Vinecour, E., and C. Fishman. 1977. *Polish Jews: The final chapter*. New York: McGraw-Hill Paperbacks.

Waters, M. C. 1990. *Ethnic options: Choosing identities in America*. Berkeley: University of California Press.

Webber, J. 1994. Modern Jewish identities. In *Jewish identities in the New Europe*, ed. J. Webber, 74–85. London: Littman Library of Jewish Civilization.

Weinbaum, L. 1998. Polish Jews: A postscript to the "final chapter"? Policy study *Issue 14*. Jerusalem: Institute of the World Jewish Congress.

Weinreich, P. 1983. Emerging from threatened identities: Ethnicity and gender in redefinitions of ethnic identity. In *Threatened identities*, ed. G. Breakwell, 149–85. Chichester: John Wiley & Sons.

Weinreich, P., V. Bacova, and N. Rougier. 2003. Basic primordialism in ethnic and national identity. In *Analysing identity: Cross-cultural, societal, and clinical contexts*, ed. P. Weinreich and W. Saunderson, 115–69. London: Routledge.

Weiss, I. 2002. Jewish Disneyland: The appropriation and dispossession of "Jewishness." *Golem European-Jewish Magazine*, No.3/6.

Wetherell, M., and J. Potter. 1992. *Mapping the language of racism: Discourse and the legitimation of exploitation*. New York: Columbia University Press.

Winnicka, E. 2003. Z kipą na głowie. *Polityka* 18:82–4.

Wiszniewicz, J. 2008 *Życie przecięte. Opowieści pokolenia Marca*. Warszawa: Czarne.

Yngvesson, B., and M. A. Mahoney. 2000. "As one should, ought and wants to be": Belonging and authenticity in identity narratives. *Theory, Culture & Society* 17(6):77–110.

Zamoyski, A. 1987. *The Polish way: A thousand-year history of the Poles and their culture*. London: John Murray.

Ziemny, A. 2000. *Resztki mniejszośći czyli Żydzi polscy dzisiaj*. Lodz: Oficyna Bibliofilow.

Zubrzycki, G. 2001. "We, the Polish Nation": Ethnic and civic visions of nationhood in post-Communist constitutional debates. *Theory and Society* 30:629–68.

Zwalman Lerner, J. Rabbi Michael Schudrich on the opportunity for renewed Jewish life in Poland. *Jewish Time Asia*. December 2010/January 2011.

INDEX